Praise for *United*

Jim Crow is dead; Jesus Christ is alive. But, like a zombie, the spirit of Jim Crow keeps walking. The answer is a gospel that is as big as the kingdom of Christ. Trillia Newbell, one of the most powerful young voices in evangelical Christianity, asks us to imagine what it would look like if reconciliation were more than rhetoric and programs but a Christ-shaped vision of an empty tomb that casts out fear, hate, and division.

RUSSELL D. MOORE
President, Ethics & Religious Liberty Commission
of the Southern Baptist Convention

Meet Trillia Newbell. Warm. Gracious. Clear. Honest. Realistic. Friendly. And eager to see the Lord's church united across ethnic lines. In *United* she has a surprisingly simple but profound idea: Racial unity happens through friendship. By the time you're finished with this book you'll think Trillia is an old friend, you'll be ready to make new friends with people not like you, and you'll want to stick with it until meaningful diversity in the body of Christ happens—all because of the gospel.

THABITI ANYABWILE
Senior Pastor, First Baptist Church of Grand Cayman

Here is a voice that brings us together, a testimony that encourages, and an aspiration that is contagious. Trillia Newbell does so many things well at the same time in this book that it is hard to articulate them all. She invites you into a fruitful conversation about the beautiful unity in multiethnic diversity that the church is meant to experience and be and manifest. Her skillfully told and deeply moving stories from the past and present are heartbreakingly real and joy-givingly hopeful. This kind of unity does not just happen; gospel unity in the church is the gift and work of God's grace by His Spirit, but it also requires a deliberate response and embrace on our part. Trillia inspires me here, and evokes in me a holy hope for what can (and should) be. I think she will for you, too.

LIGON DUNCAN, PhD
Chancellor and CEO, Reformed Theological Seminary,
John E. Richards Professor of Systematic and Historical Theology,
Senior Minister, First Presbyterian Church, Jackson, Mississippi

Trillia loves Jesus her Savior and loves the church He saved. Out of that love she tells her story and gives her call for unity in God's diverse family. Diversity is more than a subject for Trillia; it's what she has learned to live. Her words come with graciousness and grace. They are words that all of us in the church need to hear.

KATHLEEN B. NIELSON
Director of Women's Initiatives, The Gospel Coalition

United is like a picture of a wedding rehearsal dinner. Trillia shows how the table is set for a feast of grace provided by Jesus, while Christ's multiethnic bride, the church, waits for her Bridegroom. Grounded in Scripture, Trillia weaves together stories of precious friendships that are all because of the precious blood of Christ. *United* is a celebration of God's grace in reconciliation where every tribe, tongue, people, and nation are invited.

GLORIA FURMAN
Cross-cultural worker, author of *Glimpses of Grace* and *Treasuring Christ When Your Hands Are Full*

United is the story of one woman's encounters with ethnicity. It examines how ethnicity and race intersect with living out the gospel in personal relationships and in the body of Christ. The warm, conversational tone makes this book a great resource to read with another Christian who is interested in exploring the intersection between culture and faith in Christ.

KRISTIE ANYABWILE
Servant of Christ; wife of Thabiti Anyabwile,
First Baptist Church of Grand Cayman

United encourages a pursuit of unity in the midst of our diversity as believers. Trillia's personal story of fighting for unity in the body of Christ, points to a greater story of oneness that has been purchased for us by Christ's blood regardless of our ethnic, socioeconomic or cultural makeup. The message of pursuing diversity in the local gathering is timely, challenging and necessary in order to fulfill God's vision of that glorious multicultural worship service when "every tribe and language and people and nation" will be before God's throne crying out with one voice "Worthy is the Lamb who was slain!"

BLAIR LINNE
Spoken Word artist and conference speaker

Trillia writes with abundant grace, while firmly and unapologetically calling the church to examine her perception of race in the body of Christ. She asks tough questions, and encourages thoughtful introspection as she offers personal stories, biblical support, and compelling insight into historical and demographic realities. This is a theology of diversity, and it is an important read for anyone who desires to tear down the walls we've built up to keep one another at a distance.

DEIDRA RIGGS
Managing editor, *The High Calling*

Race and ethnicity are tough subjects to handle. Trillia treats them with the gravity they deserve and yet winsomely weaves in her own story of ethnic discoveries and the glories of identity in Christ. As the church continues to wrestle with realizing unity in diversity, Trillia has given us a shot of encouragement with this book. Let's thank her by reading and sharing her story.

ANTHONY CARTER
Pastor of East Point Church

United is one woman's attempt to understand issues of race and interpret her own spiritual journey through the lens of Scripture. Trillia's personal story gave me new insight into the struggles and feelings of my African-American brothers and sisters. Meanwhile, the passion with which she pursues relationships with people unlike herself gave me a renewed hope that churches in America will one day resemble more closely the church in all its multifaceted glory.

TREVIN WAX
Managing editor of The Gospel Project, author of *Clear Winter Nights, Gospel-Centered Teaching,* and *Counterfeit Gospels*

Trillia Newbell has written a heartfelt, biblical, and gospel-centered vision of racial unity in the body of Christ. Ultimately, this is Christ's vision. But Trillia has written a clear and strong witness for true Christian unity. Read this book. Share it with your friends. Pray this vision becomes a reality to the glory of God.

H.B. CHARLES, JR.
Pastor-Teacher of Shiloh Metropolitan Baptist Church

UNITED

Captured by God's Vision for Diversity

UNITED

Captured by God's Vision for Diversity

TRILLIA J. NEWBELL

MOODY PUBLISHERS

CHICAGO

Published in association with the literary agency of Wolgemuth and Associates, 8600 Crestgate Circle, Orlando, FL 32819.

Edited by Lydia Brownback
Interior design: Ragont Design
Cover design: Brock, Sharp & Associates / DBA Facout Studio
Cover image: Getty Images / #163556674
Author photo: Lillian Prince Photography

ISBN: 978-0-8024-1014-6

We hope you enjoy this book from Moody Publishers. Our goal is to provide high-quality, thought-provoking books and products that connect truth to your real needs and challenges. For more information on other books and products written and produced from a biblical perspective, go to www.moodypublishers.com or write to:

Moody Publishers
820 N. LaSalle Boulevard
Chicago, IL 60610

1 3 5 7 9 10 8 6 4 2

Printed in the United States of America

This book is dedicated to my children. I pray when you get older you would wonder why mom would write such a book. I pray God would be glorified and you would be encouraged. You are a joy to me, your mom. I love you!

CONTENTS

INTRODUCTION

IT'S SUNDAY MORNING on a crisp fall day. I've enjoyed my cup of coffee in the quiet hours of the morning and spent time praying in preparation for receiving God's spoken Word, and I now eagerly walk with my family toward the doors of our church. Pastor Lewis, a tall, dark man with a small Afro, is at the book table sharing resources with young Isamu. Isamu, which means "courageous," is from Japan and has only been in the United States for three months. He is thankful to have found a gospel-centered church and community while he studies at the local university.

Filling her travel mug with coffee is my girlfriend of over twenty-five years, Amy. Her blue eyes shine as brightly today as they did when we first started meeting together some twenty years earlier. Tuesday morning with Amy is always one of the highlights of my week—praying, studying, and learning from each other.

Mike, formerly my college pastor, and his wife, Elizabeth,

enter. Mike is part of the church's leadership team of approximately ten men whose similarities can be found only under the surface. Mike and Elizabeth adopted two African children and one from Cambodia. Their children are now grown and serving in the church.

Our church, in a mid-sized Tennessee town, is known for two things: gospel preaching and diversity. Our teachers are committed to sound preaching and sharing the good news each Sunday. No one leaves on Sunday morning without an understanding of the gospel. We take the Great Commission seriously as well, with emphasis on making disciples of *all* nations. When I stand at the front and sing with the worship team, I look out into the crowd and a sea of color. Every tribe and nation is represented, and we are all singing and worshiping the Lord, with one voice. Some can't stand still, and their worship spills out into dancing. Others simply kneel—quiet, reflective, and full of praise. It is a beautiful sight. It is a beautiful diversity.

Perhaps it's apparent simply by my descriptions of this body of believers that this is not reality; it's my dream. If you and I think about the various local churches that we've been a part of over the course of our lives, few (if any) have come even remotely close to what I've described.

The local church I truly do attend and love is a gospel-centered body that's predominantly white. And though we are continually growing in diversity, I am one of only a handful of minorities represented in my congregation. This is the reality of Sunday morning, a reality that my pastors are aware of. They would say that my vision is also their vision.

I could be easily discouraged about where we're at today, and—in those moments—I have to remind myself about the progress that has been made, most especially in broader society. We know that civil rights leaders of fifty years ago fought hard, risking life and limb to overturn the "separate but equal" Jim Crow laws. Those leaders hoped that blacks and whites would enjoy life together and that blacks would no longer be subjected to discrimination and hate crimes. This was the dream for the entire nation. Martin Luther King Jr. famously shared his dream that "one day right there in Alabama little black boys and black girls will be able to join hands with little white boys and white girls as sisters and brothers."

America has clearly come a long way since the 1960s. Our public facilities, parks, pools, and educational facilities—once segregated—are now filled with a variety of ethnic groups enjoying the benefits of their liberties. Yet our churches too often remain separate but equal. In a time of great progress, why does the church remain relatively unmoved?

Perhaps we are all tired of the conversation about race. It doesn't take much to recognize that our country continues to be divided along racial lines. Perhaps it seems that the country is moving toward unity, but it's a façade—just check your local news. And though our society may want to move on, we can't, and neither can or should the church. Maybe our churches remain segregated simply because it's comfortable. There's nothing malicious to it; we are just more comfortable with "our own." (You won't get far in this book before you'll see that I believe "our own" needs a new definition.)

But maybe it's because diversity and racial issues are scary. Talking about race and racial reconciliation can be downright terrifying. No one wants to offend, and in our politically correct society, who would blame you? If you say the wrong thing, ask the wrong question, or call someone by the wrong name, will they be angry? *Are you black or African-American? Chinese or Asian? Hispanic, Latino, or Mexican?* This is an explosive topic, and sometimes it seems that the wisest course of action is to avoid it at all costs.

John Piper recognizes the temptation to cower in fear because of previous wounds or the fear of additional wounds. He addresses this temptation in his book *Bloodlines*:

> No lesson in the pursuit of racial and ethnic diversity and harmony has been more forceful than the lesson that it is easy to get so wounded and so tired that you decide to quit. This is true of every race and every ethnicity in whatever struggle they face. The most hopeless temptation is to give up—to say that there are other important things to work on (which is true), and I will let someone else worry about racial issues. The main reason for the temptation to quit pursuing is that whatever strategy you try, you will be criticized by somebody.[1]

He's right. Pursuing diversity and racial harmony is risky business. Just look at the civil rights movement and all that its leaders endured. Chances are that those of us passionately pursuing diversity in the church won't have to face being heavily doused with fire hoses, being hauled off to jail, or worse, being killed. But we may be challenged by the laissez-faire (you know, don't fix what's not broken) or perhaps the outspoken opposer.

Either way, I join with Dr. Piper's plea: "Never quit. Change. Step back. Get another strategy. Start over. But never quit."[2]

But why? What's so vitally important that it's worth the discomfort and risks involved?

I believe it's that we can so clearly see throughout Scripture that God celebrates the diversity of His creation. He does not distinguish between races in His saving love. He created man in His own image, sent His Son to save the world, and saves anyone who believes. God calls Christians to be imitators of Christ and to walk in love. If He doesn't show partiality, neither should we.

The problem with the current church model and experience for most of us is that while we affirm these truths with our lips, Sunday morning reveals a different story.

There is a richness in knowing—*really* knowing—someone who is different from you. I bet you have (or have had) a relationship in your life that confirms the truth of this. God thought it important to let us know in His Word that every tribe and tongue and nation would be present on the last day, worshiping together. Shouldn't we desire to reflect the last day before He returns?

The reality is that we've got a problem, and we all know

it. We're not reflecting this togetherness. But knowing this problem is one thing; finding the solution is another.

But here's the good news: there is hope. Do you believe it? If not, no worries, but stay with me. I want to share my story with you, which I believe breathes hope and possibility into this general sense of skepticism related to racial reconciliation and the church.

The predominately white church I attend is a good theological fit for me and my family. We've been at the same church for a decade, but it hasn't always been easy as a minority, especially early in my experience. I feared at times being judged, and I also judged my friends in fear. It was obvious to me that I was different, and it wasn't until much later in my walk with Christ that I grew to understand that in Him I was also the same.

It won't surprise you to hear that I longed for diversity when I first started attending this body. God faithfully provided it. While it didn't come in a large wave or influx of people, small pockets of diversity developed and grew within the church. As a result, I have had the opportunity to develop rich, deep relationships with those outside of my ethnicity, including two girls who have become my best friends. Amy (white), Lillian (Chinese), and I (black) met together each week for accountability for nearly eight years. These relationships provided the friendships I needed as a young college student. But they did much more than that: they stirred our hearts and gave us a beautiful glimpse of the last day when every tongue and tribe will be present worshiping together.

Lillian, Amy, and I learned and benefited greatly from the diversity of experiences in our respective upbringings and cultures.

Our relationships sparked a renewed passion in my heart for diversity. Our friendships displayed the powerful unity found in Christ. Historical barriers were broken; thus, we reflected reconciliation. We did not hold on to the past failures and sins of our nation, thereby reflecting forgiveness. And, perhaps most importantly, we considered each other sisters in the household of Christ, reflecting acceptance and belonging.

I understand that the need for diversity and implementing the changes to make it happen can seem daunting. I desire that my story and experiences would give you a glimmer of hope. God's redeeming work through the gospel will be on full display through what I share. Jesus is the cornerstone by which all things are restored and genuine relationships are built (Ephesians 2:19–22). Racial reconciliation, harmony, and diversity aren't out of the reach of God!

God Himself created the world by the power of His voice. Surely He can do a small thing like build a church that is rich in diversity. And given our history, when it happens we will all know that it is the Lord's good doing.

So I hope you'll pull up a chair next to me as I share my personal journey, reveal the hope I have, and reflect on the goodness and grace of God. This is not another browbeating about the past. I won't be rehashing all of the history that we already know about. And neither will I discount the difficulties of genuine diversity. If diversity was easy, we wouldn't have the problems that we're confronted with today.

I'll share about the beauty of diversity that can be on display to a broken world. We will look at my life as a black female and how God fulfilled a desire of my heart through friendships. I will encourage you to know the benefits (oh, there are so many!) of being united in Christ both practically and relationally and the mutual growth acquired through fellowship with those different from you.

Dr. King hoped for little black and white children to be hand in hand, playing together. May it be brothers and sisters in Christ and in the same church. This is my story—a journey of finding faith in a world in which I am different and discovering relationships that reveal the beauty and importance of diversity in the body of Christ.

CHAPTER 1
MY NEW IDENTITY

SUMMERS GET PRETTY HOT in the South, and when you are practicing in the high school marching band after school, the ninety-degree heat can become unbearable. I played the piccolo, an instrument that resembles a miniature flute. We would stand for hours in formations with knees straight, shoulders back, chins up—all while the glaring sun was beating down on our worn-out bodies. My friend (a white male with chin-length blond hair) and I would sometimes run over to the market after band practice to grab a drink. It wasn't a far walk, and though dinnertime would be drawing close, my mouth, feeling like wool from blowing into my instrument, was desperate for refreshment. So we walked. One particular day was just like all others except for the rock that was thrown out of the window at us and the subsequent "nigger lover" epithet that followed.

This wasn't 1950 or even 1970. No, this was 1996. I grew

up in a time and a town where people knew the right things to say, but every now and then blatant, startling racism spewed out. It could be as simple as the subtle look while shopping in the mall, or as clear as the time when a woman told me it was fine for me to be her son's friend, but he was "not allowed" to date me because it wasn't "right." She wasn't concerned about protecting her son from possibly ill-advised dating behavior; rather, she was concerned that I am black.

Obviously, I couldn't help that I am a black female. That was the way the Lord chose to make me. And despite the outright opposition I encountered early in life, I chose to fully embrace who I am.

FORMING MY IDENTITY

I remember sitting on my dad's lap as a young girl while he told stories about being beaten for not standing to sing "Dixie" at a sporting event and about the torture and pain that many blacks experienced in the South. He'd end his sobering stories, which never failed to rile me up, by saying, "But, Trillia, we need to love everyone regardless of race or religion." As a result, I grew up wanting to accept everyone, despite my own rejection at times. It was how my father raised me—to love those who hate you.

As young as thirteen years old, I was drawn to watch stories about the civil rights movement and wished I could have been there, living in that time to march among the protesters. I wanted to be one of those ladies holding a sign that read, "We march for integrated schools," or doing a sit-in at a café, arms locked with other men and women and protest-ing, "Separate but equal."

But that wasn't my time period. I was born a decade after the civil rights movement had ended, and by the time I was comprehending those who came before me, we were well into the hard-rock era. Though it may be a repressed memory, I bet you remember: big hair, mismatched clothing, and scrunchies. Oh, the 80s. But I digress. I simply was born too late to be a part of the movement that meant so much to me.

Needless to say, I was incredibly thankful for the work of men like Martin Luther King Jr. Every year I would march in or watch our local Martin Luther King Day parade. I wanted to see what King dreamed of one day seeing: unity.

Though tremendous strides have been made since the civil rights movement, we can't deny that racism was still alive and well in the 80s and 90s. The most infamous act of violence and racism against an African-American during this time period was the Rodney King beating. Though none of the four Los Angeles Police Department officers involved were convicted of a race-motivated crime, the damage had been done. Citizens of Los Angeles took to the streets in savage fashion, rioting and killing.[1] The 80s and 90s were also a time when the nation was continuing to attempt to imple-ment the death of the Jim Crow separate-but-equal laws. We see it most clearly in the effort to desegregate public schools.[2]

It was against this societal backdrop that I began to de-velop a personal identity. Those were my formative years, and I had developed into a young woman who loved and embraced her blackness. I was thankful to be black, even while experiencing racist verbal attacks.

But even though I was content with my identity as a black female, I found myself in turmoil at times. I suppose there was a part of me that, while thankful for being black, was at the same time still in turmoil. You see, though I am black, I wasn't always accepted by my black peers while I was growing up. Some thought of me as a "white girl."

IDENTITY CRISIS

I'm what some people would call "proper." I speak clearly and articulate my words. I have a nondistinct accent, and well, some would just say I sound like a white girl. At least, that is what I was told in middle and high school. But my intonation and diction weren't the only things under scrutiny. I was often asked a loaded question: "Why do you act white?" I tried to not get angry, at least not in front of anyone. Instead I would come back with the quick-fire response, "What do you mean? Because I speak the way I do and I'm doing well in school, I am considered 'white'? That is just plain stupid." I had yet to learn gentleness.

This reverse racism started in middle school. Some of my black peers had accepted and adopted a stereotype for black Americans and then pressured and bullied me to fit that stereotype. It was absurd, and it communicated to me that I could not be black, smart, and articulate at the same time. It was awfully confusing for a thirteen-year-old.

These attitudes and pressures carried on into my high school years, and they're what contributed to my identity crisis. At home, I was the daughter of a black man and a black woman, the sister to black girls, the passionate civil rights activist (even though that movement was over), and the lady who sat under her father's teaching about race and racial reconciliation and longed to see racism of all kinds abolished forever. Yet at school I was labeled "white," not in color but in action. Who was I?

There wasn't much that would change this crisis in which I found myself. The confusion of being rejected by those I loved and questioned by those different from me was at times unbearable. That is, until Jesus sought me, saved me, and changed my identity.

IRRESISTIBLE GRACE

Do you ever experience something and think, *Hmmm, that must have been the Lord*?

That was my experience meeting Elizabeth. She was easily the polar opposite of me. She had blonde hair and blue eyes, a bubbly personality, and perfectly fit the descriptions "sweet" and "innocent." She was the type of gal that everyone loved and enjoyed being around. She was also a Christian.

Upon graduating from high school, I began leading cheer camps around the Southeast. I was a competitive cheerleader throughout high school, and teaching cheer camps during the summers was a perfect part-time job. Each camp session lasted for a week and consisted of at least two camp leaders and anywhere from ten to two hundred kids (with the larger camps requiring more instructors). I worked at the camps for two summers, and during the second summer, Elizabeth and I were paired together week after week. But our first meeting was the tool that God used to change the whole course of my life.

I remember it like it was yesterday. Elizabeth and I were sharing a hotel room, and it was the night before the first day of camp. She got into her pajamas, plopped down on her bed, and threw her long, straight hair back into a ponytail. I was seated on my bed, wondering if she would mind if I turned on the television, when all of a sudden she broke open her Bible. I could feel the blood rush to my face. My guard immediately went up, and I spoke frankly, "What are you doing?"

She calmly said that she was going to read her Bible. I wasn't convinced that she didn't have something else up her sleeve. I was cautious and distrusting of Elizabeth, even fearful. And I had good reason—at least I was convinced that I did.

You see, I didn't grow up in church. We were "holiday Christians." We went to church on the major holidays such as Christmas and Easter. I did become a member of a church in my junior year of high school, but it did not pan out so well. I was a teenager and had fallen romantically for an unbeliever and decided the best solution was to leave the church. But leaving was difficult because church was where I spent much of my time and where many of my friends were. Word got around that I was leaving, and it got ugly quickly.

I was pretty sure that my departure from the church was the end of my so-called Christian walk. I hated church after that experience, and the people in it nauseated me. Because of the animosity I experienced firsthand, I determined that I would distance myself as much as humanly possible from church. But that was not God's plan.

So here, at cheer camp, I found myself stuck rooming with a Christian girl for a week. Her Bible was open, ready for her to pore over the pages, and all I could think was what she might say to me and how she would scold me for leaving the church and quickly judge my life and choices.

Much to my surprise, by the end of the night we were both crying over my past church experience and my fears. And she had shared the gospel with me.

Elizabeth and I immediately became friends. But though we stayed in touch after our time together as camp counselors, it took a few years, a broken engagement, and condemnation over years of living in sin before I went to church—and stayed. I had visited her church a few times but was resistant to regular attendance. But after my engagement ended, I knew that was where I needed to be. The breakup felt like I was in one of those natural-disaster moments when everyone turns to God, but this time I didn't turn away from Him when the dust cleared. I could fight the Lord all I wanted, but His irresistible grace had taken my heart captive.

I will never forget the day I finally gave my life to the Lord. It was a Sunday morning, and I hadn't been back to the church in probably a year. While singing the hymn "Rock of Ages," the Lord began to soften my heart, and He revealed His grace to me. After the service, I sought out Elizabeth and two other friends who prayed for me and guided me into new life. I was saved.

My rebirth was a time of rejoicing. The change in my heart was radical. And the transformation of my desires was almost instantaneous. God had taken out a heart of stone and replaced it with a beating heart of flesh, and it was on fire. I wanted nothing more than to share the good news with others. I was a new creation.

IN CHRIST

I love conversion stories. Remembering my own brings tears to my eyes and fills my heart with gladness. I rejoice when I hear about a man steeped in the drug culture who turns from his ways, or a woman who grew up in a religious home and finally comes to understand that her salvation is through faith alone by grace alone. All stories of God's redeeming love are amazing, but the one that always moves me deeply is the conversion of Paul.

We first meet Paul (known at that time as Saul) at the stoning of Stephen (Acts 7:58). Saul was respected among Hebrews and in Jerusalem. By his own account, he had earnestly obeyed the law and was of noble blood: "Circumcised on the eighth day, of the people of Israel, of the tribe of Benjamin, a Hebrew of Hebrews; as to the law, a Pharisee; as to zeal, a persecutor of the church; as to righteousness under the law, blameless" (Philippians 3:5–6). He went through homes and imprisoned men and women, ravaged the church, and approved of killings and beatings of followers of Jesus. He was the last person anyone would have thought would one day also be a follower of Jesus Christ, let alone one of the greatest missionaries Christianity has ever known. But when God saves, there's a radical transformation.

Paul's conversion was quite dramatic. First, a light flashed from heaven, and the voice of the Lord began to speak. Paul went blind, and this independent, fierce leader of persecution needed assistance from his buddies to walk him to Damascus. Once there, he didn't eat and remained blind for three days until Ananias showed up. Ananias was there only because Jesus had directly commanded him to go to Saul, lay hands on him, and restore his sight. Ananias was scared— and rightly so. Saul was well-known and feared by the early church because of his zealous persecution. Nevertheless, Ananias obeyed and went to meet with Saul. When he laid hands upon him, something "like scales" fell from Saul's eyes, and his vision returned. Immediately Saul was baptized, and immediately after that he began to proclaim Christ in the synagogues (Acts 9:1–22).

Our conversion experiences may not be as dramatic as Paul's. Okay, they probably aren't close to being as dramatic. But the results are the *exact* same. When Paul was converted, his old self was completely gone; he was a new man (Colossians 3:10). John Piper explains it like this: "In conversion, our old self died and was laid aside with its impulses and drives and values and loves and convictions. And a new self was created by God. This is called in other places 'the new birth' or being born again (John 3:3; 1 Peter 1:3)."[3]

With this new birth comes a new identity. We no longer live for ourselves—and we are no longer ourselves. We are a new creation. Paul wrote about this new creation in Galatians: "I have been crucified with Christ. It is no longer I who live, but Christ who lives in me. And the life I now live in the flesh I live by faith in the Son of God, who loved me and gave himself for me" (Galatians 2:20). Being identified with Christ means full and free acceptance by God, the ability to approach a holy God, no condemnation, complete forgiveness, righteousness before God, and presentation to God one day as blameless and perfect. Now, that's amazing grace!

What I discovered as I grew in my Christian faith was that my identity is not solely that I am a black female, nor is it dependent on what others think of me. My identity is in Christ.

When I find my identity in Christ and not in outward appearance, there's satisfaction. I'm satisfied in Him because He loves me. Elyse Fitzpatrick puts it this way: "I don't need to be concerned with these things at all, because I've been given assurances that eclipse all else. I've been given the God-Man, Jesus Christ, who is able to save me to the uttermost and who is living, right now, in this very instant, to make intercession for me before his Father (Heb. 7:25)."[4]

As Christians we have been given the God-man! Jesus—fully God and fully man—is ours. There isn't a love that can trump this. When God looks at us, He no longer sees the sin that so ensnared us before salvation; He now sees us clothed in Christ's righteousness. He looks at us and sees His Son's perfect obedience. He sees beauty. God sees us in Christ.

God wrecked my identity crisis. *I am in Christ.*

It was as if all the knowledge that was in my head had become a reality. I got it. I finally understood that my identity is not my own—my identity isn't about me. But it's one thing to know this truth; it's another to understand it and have opportunities to apply it. I am thankful that I have found those opportunities within my church and throughout my walk with Christ.

> **BEING BLACK IS A PART OF MY IDENTITY. BUT IT ISN'T *MY* *ENTIRE IDENTITY.***

NO LONGER JUST A BLACK GIRL

As I reflect on my conversion, the effects stagger me. Understanding that my identity is no longer in my blackness, what I do and don't do, or how others view me has been incredibly freeing. This knowledge allows me to enjoy my relationship with Christ and my relationships with others. It has also provided me the opportunity to enjoy my identity as a black woman in a better way.

I am made by God in His image. God created me, all of me (Psalm 139:13). I can celebrate my differences and embrace all that God has for me because I am His creation. My identity is no longer in crisis. I am black to His glory. I was created by God for a purpose. I am in Christ by His grace, and all Christians can justly, because of Christ, say the same.

And though the new identity now trumps all other identity claims on my life, one fact remains—to those who see me, I am black.

First impressions matter. Before I open my mouth, people have summed me up (consciously or otherwise) to varying degrees. If someone were to describe me without knowing me or speaking to me, they might say, "You are a female, short in stature, and have dark hair, brown eyes, and, well, are black." People are not truly "color blind." Being black is a part of my identity. But it isn't *my entire identity*.

After my conversion, it was apparent to me that being black isn't my entire identity. I knew it wasn't even my *first* identity. And though the richness of that truth took some time to sink in, I had become first a Christian, then a black woman. Nevertheless, I found myself in a predominantly white church—in Christ yet still different. I immersed myself in this church, and even though I was one of only a handful of minorities there, my minority status didn't matter to me at first. I was so overcome by the work God had done in my heart that nothing else really mattered.

My identity crisis was over, but a new war in my heart began. I was different, which was plain to me, and I was occasionally innocently reminded of it. My new identity didn't erase the obvious cultural and physical differences between me and my white brothers and sisters in Christ. We *were* different, although the same in Christ. Our differences were clearly felt, and as a result, I would at times feel lonely, isolated, and even fearful. My identity was secure, but there was something missing in my fellowship, a longing deep in my heart that became clear over time.

CHAPTER 2
MY WHITE CHURCH

I LOVE A GOOD SNOWFALL. It's rare that I get to experience it living in the South, but when I do, I often run outside like a young child and let the snowflakes fall on my face. It's beautiful. Soft, gentle, white delicate pieces of frozen water falling gently on my face as I look up into the heavens, wondering how God could create such a phenomenon—snow.

Snowflakes are said to be unique; no one snowflake resembles another. The white flakes are created with intricate designs, yet, because of their general color, they appear to be all the same. Every once in a while, however, I've noticed that a snowflake will catch the reflection of the light around it and exhibit a varying hue. The colorful snowflake clearly stands out as it falls among the other flakes.

At times in my church experience, I felt like I was a part of a great snowstorm: I was surrounded by numerous other snowflakes, unique in character and gifts, yet I was that one snowflake that reflected the light of its surroundings differently as it fell with the rest. My reflection was of God's image, like all mankind, yet still distinct in color from the other members. I guess you could say that I quite literally reflected a different hue—and it stood out.

Still filled with joy and understanding that I had become a new creation, I continued attending the predominately white church where I first heard the gospel. As I mentioned, that simply didn't matter to me at first. Upon salvation there was one thing on my mind: *How do I know this God of my rebirth?* I was aware of my deep need for forgiveness. I knew I had sinned. I understood that my sin was justly deserving of God's wrath. When God also revealed that my sin could be forgiven and *was* forgiven, I had to know more about Him. It was this desire to know God more that motivated me to keep attending my church.

That was about thirteen years ago. The church was a small congregation with about two hundred members. It wasn't a fancy or impressive place to visit. Attenders met in a school, my high school alma mater, to be exact, which made for an odd mix of embarrassment and excitement— embarrassment because of old school pictures of me hanging in various parts of the building that I only hoped no one would see, and excitement because every now and then I'd see someone that I had gone to school with.

What made the church special was the warmth of the people. I found myself drawn to the hospitable women hanging on to their babies with one hand and their Bibles with the other while asking me questions about my life. And then there were the zealous college students—who knew young people could be so excited about God? I didn't know, but they were. I was just as young, so their enthusiasm for the Lord intrigued me.

The pastors sought to preach the gospel each week. Members were encouraged to dive into books on theology and doctrine. I hadn't experienced many churches. I didn't grow up in church. The one church I had attended didn't have a bookstore, and rarely did the pastor reference authors, theology, or doctrine, so the idea of Christian books or even theology was very new to me. These aspects of the church were compelling. There was so much to learn about God and various ways to get to know Him. Ultimately all of those resources and the methodology the pastors applied led me to want to read the most important book available for knowing God: the Bible.

It wasn't long before I began to hear words such as *sanctification, justification, propitiation,* and *sovereignty.* I had never known that Jesus' death was a substitutionary sacrifice. I didn't know that I deserved wrath, but that He had borne it. I didn't realize that upon believing in faith, I would receive His righteousness. Most of all, I didn't know that it was free. I didn't realize that it is by grace that we are saved and not a result of works (Ephesians 2:8). I longed to learn and read in order to more deeply understand this God who had redeemed me, and with the assistance of books and God's Word, I began to develop a theological foundation by which to walk out my new faith.

My new identity in Christ continued to trump the lack of diversity in the church. I immersed myself in the life of the church, and even though I was one of only a handful of minorities, it didn't matter. *And*, I reasoned, *why would it?* God had reconciled me to Himself, and I was focused on learning much about Him.

So I settled in, became a member, and began to serve on ministry teams. Serving in my church was easy, not in concept but in need. It was a young church at the time, maybe only ten years old. Each Sunday, teams of people would come early to set everything up, from the stage to placing signs for children's ministry, including all the materials needed for the classes. There were needs, and I was excited to find my place. The concept of using my abilities in the service of others was a new and striking experience. Previously, I had seen my abilities as talents—talents that were meant for *me* to use for *my own* glory. I discovered that God didn't simply give me talents; He gave me gifts that were meant to be poured out for the benefit of others. Little did I know that God would also use my history and perspective to serve the church.

I began attending small-group meetings. I went to our singles ministry events and eventually to our college ministry events. Wonderful friendships developed, and within a few years I applied for an internship with our college ministry. I served in that capacity, leading women's Bible studies and evangelizing at our local university. I knew at that moment that I loved serving women. I will forever be grateful for the chance I had to encourage and pray with young ladies as they divulged their struggles and fears, often with tear-filled eyes, and seeing the power of the gospel regenerate hearts of stone to hearts of flesh.

There was a sweetness in my church that I thank God for even today. It is where I came to know Christ and where my relationship with Him flourished. Yet the longer I remained a member, the more I sensed the cultural differences. I was still like the snowflake free-falling with its varying hue, unsure if I was fully a part of the whole.

THE LONELY SNOWFLAKE

Have you ever experienced that odd sense that you're alone even when you're in the midst of hundreds of people? I'm all too familiar with that strange sensation, and I became increasingly aware of it as my time at the church lengthened.

Loneliness can seem irrational sometimes. I was rarely alone—almost never—yet at times within the church I would find myself feeling completely alone. In a way, it was true: I was practically alone in regard to ethnicity. I was one of only ten to twenty African-Americans in my church when I first began attending. (Yes, I just counted on my fingers to make sure I got that right!) I was the only black female church member who attended the college ministry, and there were no black males. There were an underwhelming three black males in the singles ministry and, again, no females at the time.

Now, this is not to say that my church didn't care or attempt to invite minorities. Actually, they had a deep desire to invite people from all backgrounds and ethnicities. And, more than that, they had a desire to see all people come to know Jesus Christ as their Lord and Savior. The obstacle we faced is that we lived in a predominantly white city. My church simply reflected the community in which we lived.[1] (I address these potential obstacles and others in chapter 8.)

Yet I wasn't the only one who realized that I was the only one. Curiosity got the best of some of my friends, and they inquired about my hair, about how my skin would react in the sun, and about politics. Some assumed I was a Democrat because I am black. Far from being offended, I loved answering these various questions because my blackness is an important aspect of who I am. So answering the curious questions of others was truly my joy. And, by the grace of God, I was never offended. No one asked me questions to (further) isolate me but only to know more about my culture.

At the same time, although the questions were innocent and well-intentioned, I began to feel uneasiness about those obvious differences and what that meant in terms of relationships, activities, and even the music that I desired for worship.

I remember having a meeting with my pastor and the interns in the church as the pastor prayed through how to serve the few blacks attending, and there was another meeting with a pastor and a group of church members who had a desire to see it become multicultural. I recall it was more like a party of maybe twenty people and less like a meeting. There was homemade smoked barbeque pork ribs and all the Southern fixins you can imagine. We met to strategize ways to reach more minorities in the community and simply to pray. I'm not sure that anything was implemented from that meeting, but it was unifying to be united in prayer with so many.

These experiences exemplify the body of Christ at work. We were all seeking to learn from each other and serve one another in love. There was prayer and effort and thoughtfulness. But often the fears I experienced were overwhelming, and they were generally fought in secret and silence. I was silent because my fears seemed deeply personal. At times I was ashamed and even embarrassed by what I was afraid of, namely, rejection.

FEAR OF REJECTION

God has a way of revealing our hearts to us. He began the process of revealing my fear of rejection by giving me a desire for children. You see, I had no desire for children prior to becoming a Christian. When I became a Christian, one of the many works God did in my heart was to change my view of children. Prior to salvation, I imagined children as a burden to my ambitions. I had no desire for them. I had set my sights on law school and work in Washington, DC. I couldn't imagine pursuing those "dreams" and caring for kids. But as the Lord worked in my heart, I grew to recognize the blessing of children (Psalm 127:3). I also began to long for marriage, yet I didn't want to get married just to have children. I also longed for companionship, as do so many young adults entering that stage of life right out of college. But I feared that the relationship I desired could not be met in my white church.

My parents had raised me to believe all people are the same in regard to value and worth, and therefore I was always open to marrying whomever the Lord would have for me, regardless of ethnicity. But throughout my childhood I was often told by others (black and white) that interracial marriage is wrong. As I became more and more aware of my differences, I also became fearful that I would experience the same push-back from the members of my congregation.

I wish that I had lived out those few years before graduation and right after college full of peace and trusting in God, but I didn't. Many young girls fight the idol of marriage, and I count myself among this number.[2] So I had to fight against desiring marriage too much along with a general fear that I might not be accepted by a man because of my ethnicity. And because of my past experiences, I feared that if I were asked to be in a relationship, the man's family would not accept and welcome me.

My fears were many regarding marriage as I looked into what I perceived as limited opportunities to get to know other men in my church. I didn't express my anxiety often. It seemed to be a battle that no one would understand. Most of my friends weren't battling this. They were *white* in a *white* church with *white* men. Sure, they struggled with the desire and longing for marriage and the need to wait, but they didn't have the added fear of wondering if they'd be accepted due to their skin appearance.

On top of my struggles concerning marriage, I experienced the simple desire to be accepted in general. The ladies in the church with whom I became friends already had deep friendships with each other, had been roommates, and in many ways simply didn't need another friend. My new girlfriends were very loving and evangelistic, so I never felt completely unwanted—just never fully a part. I imagine many people struggle with feeling not a part of a group when attending a new church. I am confident that my feelings of exclusion were not because my girlfriends had issues with race. On the contrary, they never once made me feel that my being black was a factor in our friendships. Yet because of my past experiences with racism, my fear of rejection and desire for acceptance were compounded even with my friends.

I longed to be accepted. I wanted to fit in. I found myself craving the approval of the church members. I desired their approval and tried to cram myself into a culture that in many ways was not my own. From the contemporary Christian worship music played with electric and acoustic guitars to the activities such as the Country Boy Olympics, I didn't always relate fully. Given my need for acceptance, I never expressed much concern about the culture (out loud).

I distinctly remember one day receiving a compilation CD from our worship pastor to listen to and practice at home and being slightly shocked by the amount of gospel music we were learning. As I listened intently to the music, trying to pick out the alto section among the multitude of voices and musical parts that often embody gospel music, I felt my heart swell with thanksgiving. I hadn't realized until that moment just how much I identified with that genre of music. This seemingly insignificant event triggered the realization that I had a longing for a more culturally diverse environment. It wasn't enough to drive me out of the church, because I loved that congregation, the teaching, and my pastoral team, but it was a seed that God slowly grew and nurtured.

FEAR OF MAN AND ACCEPTANCE BY GOD

Wanting to be included or a part of a community isn't inherently bad, for God made us to be communal. We are born through a relationship with another. We attend church with a community of believers. God Himself is communal—three in one.

But my desires for acceptance and approval dulled the powerful effect of the gospel that at first caused awe and amazement. The fact that I was an accepted and loved new creation had all but disappeared from my view. It's as if I had forgotten that truth for a season. I had quickly become much more aware of my differences from others than of my sameness in Christ.

At the time, I didn't fully understand the significance of the rebirth and what it meant to be in community with others as a new creation. All I knew was that during those times when I wondered if I would be left out of an event or would ever marry or felt awkward doing an activity such as the Country Boy Olympics, I felt profoundly "different."

I am thankful that God began to reveal to me that I

needed to fight a different fight. I had a battle to fight in my soul. I ultimately needed to find my acceptance, identity, and security in Him and not in man.

Though my struggle was with cultural and physical differences, we can all feel this sense of fear of rejection at times. Think about sending off a college application and needing to wait for someone else to make a decision as to whether you are accepted. I remember trying out for the cheerleading squad and feeling that I might get sick to my stomach waiting on the list of squad members to be pinned up on the board. These are simply examples of the fear of rejection we experience, often when we must wait for an answer. The fear I have in mind is different. I'm talking about what the Bible calls "the fear of man." Proverbs addresses this fear: "The fear of man lays a snare, but whoever trusts in the Lord is safe" (Proverbs 29:25).

The fear of man is a preoccupation with what others think of you. The fear of man can lead you to do things that you would not normally do. We see this grievous sin played out in the life of Peter, Jesus' disciple who walked behind at a distance as the officers carried Jesus off to be slaughtered. After they had seized Jesus, Peter had three chances to proclaim Christ, yet he denied Him each time (Luke 22:54–62). Jesus had predicted Peter's denial, but Peter had insisted it would never happen (Matthew 26:33–35). After the third denial Peter wept. He knew that at those moments, he loved the approval of man more than he loved the Man, his friend, who in a moment's time would die in his place.

Like Peter, when I fear man I'm really denying Christ. That may seem extreme, but think of it this way: I am essentially elevating the thoughts, attitudes, and acceptance of others so much that it rules me, therefore diminishing the rule, authority, and opinion of God in my life. There is a great danger in caring this much about what others think. And God was incredibly gracious to reveal the error of my thinking and the sinful pattern in my heart.

It might be easy to assume that in order to reverse the effects of the fear of man in my life, I must put on pride and build a security in myself. You might think that I must love myself more or be stronger in who I am as a black woman. The world's prescription for the cure of the fear of man is to find ways to be proud of oneself and find security in and through the self. Quotes like "Love yourself," or "Believe in yourself," or even the sweet but theologically lame quote widely attributed to Walt Disney, "If you can dream it, you can do it," are all focused on self. But God says that the opposite of the fear of man isn't finding security and pride in oneself. No, it's placing one's trust and security in Him. God's promise is that those who place their trust in Him will be safe. And the writer of Proverbs describes God as a strong tower that the righteous run into and are safe (Proverbs 18:10).

God wanted me not to think more highly of myself and thus less of the members of my church. He wasn't calling me to be brought high. He was drawing me to Himself and saying, *Come to Me, fearful saint, and I will give you security in Me.* He wanted me to think more highly of *Him*, thereby lowering my desire and need for the acceptance of others. If I'm accepted by Him, and if I understand what that acceptance means, then I no longer need to be concerned about being accepted by others.

So what does this acceptance by God look like for you and me? At the time I knew myself to be a new creation, but God was revealing to me the life-altering truth that I am also His daughter. Paul assures us of our new bloodline when he writes, "The Spirit himself bears witness with our spirit that we are children of God, and if children, then heirs—heirs of God and fellow heirs with Christ, provided we suffer with him in order that we may also be glorified with him" (Romans 8:16–17).

Whoa! That's right; I'm a child of God and a fellow heir with Christ—amazing! And this is not because of anything I did or could ever do. God's acceptance and adoption of me are all His own doing. And the beauty of this adoption is that our color does not affect His decision to adopt us. Think about how beautiful and wonderful it is when people adopt a child. We rejoice knowing that an orphan who was once abandoned or neglected now has a home. That is beautiful, and even still it doesn't compare to the adoption we experience as believers. Unlike a parent who prayerfully considers whom to adopt based on country, ethnicity, and even physical limitations, God chooses us based purely on His mercy and love. Despite who we are, God still chooses to save us. There isn't anything in us that governs His adoption (Ephesians 1:5). For we know that there is no distinction between men; all have sinned, all need the redemption that can come only through Christ, and God justifies freely all who come to Him (Romans 3:22–31; 10:12). Every tongue, every tribe, every nation—all those who believe are adopted by God through Christ.

Our adoption is a glorious mystery. Paul continues to help us grasp it in Galatians: "But when the fullness of time had come, God sent forth his Son, born of woman, born under the law, to redeem those who were under the law, so that we might receive adoption as sons. And because you are sons, God has sent the Spirit of his Son into our hearts, crying, 'Abba! Father!' So you are no longer a slave, but a son, and if a son, then an heir through God" (Galatians 4:4–7).

God's great love and redemption through the blood of Christ bought my salvation *and* my acceptance by God as His daughter. What other acceptance do I need? No other acceptance. But it's hard to believe, isn't it? I live and walk out my life tangibly with people. I communicate and hear the audible words of people. When I need something immediately, I call up someone and ask for it. Even though I know that the Most High accepts me, there's a real fight against the flesh, because I am in the flesh. We have an incredibly limited view. And we spend our entire lives earning things. If we do well in school, we earn good grades. If we apply for a job, we get hired, or perhaps we are rejected. We are all judged, almost daily, based on other's presumptions of us. But when considering us, God looks only to His Son.

Nevertheless, this work and revelation didn't happen

overnight. It took a few years to understand that God accepts me, and therefore I needed to trust Him and draw near to Him and fight the temptation to want acceptance from others. The fight started with a realization that God loves me. It seems so simple, but the love of God is truly profound. His love is so great and costly, and it was ultimately displayed on the cross. We've grown familiar with John 3:16: "For God so loved the world, that he gave his only Son, that whoever believes in him should not perish but have eternal life." We know this Scripture. It's on billboards and religious paraphernalia. But it is the Scripture we need to fight against the fear of man in our hearts. If God so loved me, to the point of death, why would I desire the approval of anyone? If God is for me, which He has proven He is, who can be against me? (Romans 8:31). Isn't His love enough? It is more than enough!

God was faithful to help me believe that what He says in His Word, He means. As I began to trust Him, I simultaneously began to fear less. The fear of man began to subside in my heart. It became easier to be involved in and to *enjoy* my church.

My fear of rejection wasn't something that could be perceived (at least, I don't think so). Much of it was hidden away in my heart. Although sin and temptations are difficult to confess, I have benefited firsthand from the promises of 1 John 1:9: He is faithful to forgive and to purify. You might have a black friend or parishioner who is struggling with similar fears. Our churches should have environments in which freely sharing struggles is not only welcomed but also accepted. In other words, we can say that we have environments where people are welcome to share and then *harshly* judge or critique the very sharing that we have encouraged. We should lovingly hear the concerns, failures, and confessions of others and offer wisdom, love, guidance, and encouragement—even when we disagree. I was thankful that I could eventually confess my fear of man to trusted friends without the fear of rejection that had once paralyzed me. I was also thankful for the meetings that allowed members of our congregation to share openly and freely about felt needs and desires. Isn't that part of being in community, having the ability to communicate openly and freely in love?

God doesn't waste our experiences, does He? I wasn't growing in Christ despite my environment; I was growing *because* of my environment. God was teaching me how to trust Him, seek Him, learn from Him, and find my ultimate satisfaction in Him. Like a gentle father, God was holding my hand and caring for me as I sought to gain faith and understanding about my future. He was giving me peace.

Yet throughout this process, my desire for diversity didn't dissipate, and that was okay. I needed to fight the temptation to care about what others thought of me, but that didn't mean that my desires for a diverse environment were wrong. On the contrary, as I began to read and understand God's Word, it became clear to me that built into the pages of His Word is a theology of diversity. I began to see that my desire for diversity wasn't only okay—it also made sense, given the manner by which God speaks in the Word about tongues, tribes, ethnicity, and ultimately diversity, both indirectly and directly.

CHAPTER 3
LONGING FOR DIVERSITY

BEING ONE OF THE FEW BLACK Christians was the first driving force behind my desire for diversity in my church. As I felt increasingly different, I simultaneously desired a more multiethnic congregation. Even though I loved my church and enjoyed being a part of its life and ministry, I couldn't help but at times feel weary of being *that* snowflake.

My eagerness for multiethnic relationships wasn't new to me. I have a long history of promoting (or at the very least discussing) diversity in whatever sphere I'm present. It started first with a lesson on the hard and painful realities many blacks faced during the civil rights movement.

Growing up, my father frequently shared stories about the civil rights movement with us girls. I remember a particularly memorable story that he told when I was about fifteen years old. My father was an animated and confident man, so when he spoke, we listened. Because I had such a deep respect for him, the difficult things he endured as a young man just seemed unimaginable.

One particular story, which I briefly noted earlier, struck me hard. My father had the opportunity to attend a conservative college in the South. One day at a college football game, he refused to stand while "Dixie,"[1]—the song made popular after the Civil War and sung by artists in blackface—was being played. I remember crying as he described being taunted and beaten for his refusal to stand. This occurred in the 60s, right after the civil rights movement had come to a climax. I was horrified by the thought of my father enduring such pain and suffering—a man, a grown man, I respected so very much. It seemed as though someone were taking part of his manhood from him while he recounted the story to his daughters. Of course, he knew that he had adoring girls who respected him all the more when they realized that he not only endured but also forgave. He was teaching us invaluable lessons.

Though my father didn't mince words about the horrors of our past, he was never graphic. Most of the images of the physical effects of racism I had seen were from the days of slavery. And naïvely I assumed that because slavery had ended, and because America has laws that supposedly protect us, horrific acts of violence are fewer. I imagine I'm not the only one who thinks such a thing. Unless you are in the throes of a movement or in the Deep South, it is easy to fall into the naïve assumption that freedom means equality (unless you yourself are or were at one time racist). And as a young child, all things seem somewhat of a utopia. My parents were protective. I was aware of lynching, cross burnings, and beatings, but it wasn't until college, when I viewed a documentary about the civil rights movement, that I fully grasped the horror and terror many blacks had felt during that time.

It was my freshman year at the University of Tennessee (UT) when I grasped it. I was required to go to the library to watch a documentary describing the events leading up to the civil rights movement. I thought I knew. I thought I understood. I am black, and I had experienced racism. But it wasn't until I watched this film in which a young black boy, probably about eight years old, was dragged to death behind a pickup truck, that I finally knew. I got it. I understood the fight. Though I had experienced racism, I had never known this. There was something about seeing the graphic and gory images of his disfigured, lifeless face. I couldn't imagine adults senselessly killing a young boy, especially in such a brutal way. And if my memories serve me right, his death was a result of talking to a white girl. Shame.

My heart began to pound out of my chest. I was angry. I was angry that America had allowed slavery to be a catalyst for such evil and hate. I was angry that anyone would feel justified in doing something so horrific to such a young boy. I was only ten years older than the young boy; it wasn't a stretch to think that this could have been me had I lived at that time. I read more and more stories of rape and beatings, evil murders of other young men such as Emmett Till, and even now as I think about it, my eyes begin to water with tears and my heart grows heavy.

From my freshman-year vantage point, society had come a long way, it seemed, from those days, though we'd continue to hear of wretched stories of racism. Being beaten, tortured, and lynched wasn't, however, something most blacks were concerned about daily. My newfound sentiments compelled me to begin thinking of ways this eighteen-year-old could bridge the racial gap at my university.

A year later I found myself as the codirector of diversity affairs for our student government association. One way I thought I would be able to promote diversity was through openly discussing race and racism among the student body. I had attended a discussion of this nature once before at UT and reported on it for our school newspaper, *The Daily Beacon*. When I started the position, I expanded on what I had seen and began hosting campus-wide events at which students could come and discuss topics on diversity, racism, and unity. At the time, the university had twenty-six thousand students, with approximately 6 percent of those students being minorities (nonwhite). These talks seemed to be a practical way to bridge the gap.

What was interesting about these talks, and I would argue remains to be the case, is that people are confused and quite unsure about race—how to approach it and confused about people in general. As with most aspects of life and issues of race in particular, you don't know unless you ask. So these talks provided a nonthreatening environment to ask anything. Now, don't get me wrong: conversations became heated, as accusations were typically shared at one point or another. But overall there seemed to be a mystery about ethnicities and experience that plagued people. Yet as they asked questions, it was like scales falling off eyes and weight rolling off shoulders. People were being enlightened. They were gaining understanding. This is the fruit of asking rather than assuming—we gain understanding.

While this was only a small effort that lasted one year, it changed my heart forever. I was no longer simply angry and hurt about the racism that I had experienced or had seen through the documentary. I now saw it for what it was at the core—hate. This revelation wouldn't be biblically grounded in me until later, but it was a start. I was beginning to get a grasp of the human condition—that our hearts are hardwired for sin, so apart from Christ we are capable of all sorts of evil.

As I continued to develop in college, my main goal took a change from "Let's make the world a better place through diversity" to "I need to be as successful as possible." I had been told growing up that I would need to work hard, much harder, to make it in a world run by white people. At the time, I felt I was doubly oppressed. I was a minority through race and unequal as a woman. As a woman, I would need to be able to challenge men and fight for rights, and as a minority I would need to do the same.

And in looking at our history, it makes sense. In 1619 a little colony in Virginia took in the first slaves in America. That move would decidedly set the history of racial divide, bigotry, and inequality in America for the next four centuries. By the mid-1800s, abolitionists were gaining steam, and the Union victory of the American Civil War would free the nation's four million slaves.[2] Though freed, the fight for true freedom wasn't over. Many Southern states instituted the Jim Crow Law separating blacks and whites from public facilities and schools. While this was happening, another movement was brewing.

Women were growing increasingly wary of their position in society. Susan B. Anthony pioneered the women's suffrage movement that would lead to the adoption of the Nineteenth Amendment (1920), allowing women to vote and paving the way for the feminist movement of the twentieth century.

But through it all, there remained one section of the population that was largely ignored—the black female. Besides the popular Rosa Parks, can you name any black female who fought for the rights of women and blacks during the suffrage movement or the civil rights movement? It's hard to think of any others, but they were there.

Writer Lynne Olson documented the historical accounts of black females during these movements and makes mention of the hardship they endured:

> At a time when white women were treated, at least in public, with exaggerated politeness and respect, black women, no matter how cultured or educated or well dressed, were thrown out of theaters, tossed off trains and streetcars, pushed off sidewalks, roughed up by conductors and policemen.

Unfortunately, it was much worse than being merely roughed up. She continues:

> The flagrant humiliation of black women was tied to the widespread belief, stemming from the days of slavery, that they did not deserve respect or consideration, because they were sexual wantons who led men astray. . . . In the late 1800s, Southern blacks began their great migration to the North—200,000 alone between 1890 and 1910—to seek better economic opportunities and to flee Jim Crow. According to historian Darlene Clark Hine, many of the black women who left the South did so for yet another reason—to escape sexual exploitation and the possibility of rape.[3]

I share this brief history, not because I now feel like I am a victim but because my mother's generation lived this life. This was her reality. Her mother and her mother's mother were immersed in the struggles detailed above. My father's mother and her mother's mother experienced the same hardships. Though I was not born in that era, I was reminded of the struggle as a young woman, and it is that history that guided me to my adult years.

Understanding my history gives a foundation and texture to understanding the motivation behind my desire to be successful, as the world would define it. Education, well-paying jobs, and good social positioning were important. So

I took to heart the challenge to be successful, not to prove that I could do anything my fellow white men and women could do but to prove that *anyone could be successful.*

I vividly remember bawling in one of my upper-level political science classes when I heard a young, white man proclaim that blacks only achieve because of affirmative action. I had recently been accepted into two law schools, and I had an excellent grade-point average; it never once crossed my mind that I might have been accepted only because I am black. I shared this with my classmate and the rest of the class. What had been a desire for diversity turned into a desire for achievement and, in some ways, to prove that, yes, a black woman can do well. And I did do well.

Perhaps my past achievement and pride (sometimes good, often rooted in self-glorification) is what kept me silent in my church for so many years. I didn't want to be seen as someone who struggled with rejection. When you've been taught to achieve and do well and fight for rights, it's hard to face the fact that you actually care about what others think of you. I had built up a wall and confidence, but under it all I just really wanted to be accepted. I wanted to be understood. So as I began to understand my heart from a biblical perspective, I was shocked to see that all the confidence and pride that I had built as safety armor was falling off. They were crumbling, and all I had left was fear. Underneath my confidence was a little girl scared of being rejected by people.

STILL LONGING

But here I was, in my church—having longed for diversity and understanding before—trying to navigate my feelings once again and fighting the fear in my heart. Though the gospel gripped my heart, there remained something missing. I knew the truth about the gospel and about the racial-barrier-smashing effect it has in the life of a believer, yet I still longed for a diverse environment.

While it might have looked as though I was discontented, I wasn't. I loved my church, and I wasn't looking for a different congregation. I didn't want to flee my church as my desire for diversity grew—that action would only make it less diverse. I wasn't grumbling about these unmet desires. I plunged into church life and became an active member. I loved the people there, and I wanted to wait on the Lord to bring more diversity. Then God began to develop in me a biblical theology for diversity and a conviction that diversity is actually a gift of God's grace for the benefit of all people.

I was formulating those ideas and hiding them away in my heart. Besides those few meetings with my church members about the desire for diversity in the church, I had never expressed how I felt. Even in those meetings, I never spoke about my personal feelings, partly because of my fear of rejection but also because much of our meeting time was not about personal stories but about brainstorming ideas for growth. Actually, I wasn't sure at the time that I'd even know how to articulate what I felt. It wasn't until many years later, when my senior pastor asked me to review John Piper's book

Bloodlines, that it dawned on me that I had kept all these feelings and concerns completely to myself. On occasion I shared a few things with my best friend, but even then my thoughts were not fully formulated, and I wasn't sure that anyone would truly "get it."

Dr. Piper's book solidified everything I had ever thought. It put words and life to my inner yearnings. I was floored, really, and was ready to share my thoughts and concerns with my pastors. From *Bloodlines* came an email to my pastors sharing my suppressed views and other things the Lord was revealing to me for the church. The email evolved into a blog post, and from there I discovered I wasn't alone in my concerns. Women emailed me, wrote me notes, and sent me messages to let me know that they too had a longing for diversity and understanding.

If I can point out one impact of the book *Bloodlines*, it's that it brought the topic of race and the church back into the forefront of the evangelical conversation. Conversations about race and church life have been on the rise since its publication. I've seen it through Dr. Piper's organization, Desiring God; through young authors such as Trevin Wax; and through Southern Baptist leaders such as Russell Moore. And if that weren't proof enough that there is a greater conversation about race and church happening, it's undeniable that the 2012 election of Reverend Fred Luter Jr., the first African-America president for the Southern Baptist Convention, has had an impact on the climate and conversation.

People are talking, and this is a good thing.

Whatever the impetus, I'm thankful. I'm thankful that there seems to be an open dialogue about race, particularly as it relates to blacks and whites worshiping together. With that said, even after reading books, articles, and blog posts, I continued to find one element of the black experience missing—the black *female* experience.

When my pastor kindly asked me to read and review *Bloodlines* for him, his interest wasn't merely in the book; he also wanted to know how he could serve his parishioners better, which I continue to applaud and am most grateful for. Piper's book opened my eyes to remember and reevaluate my experience at my local church and in my Christian walk. Being black, female, and Reformed is one of those unique blends.[4] I am a rare breed. But it was almost as if I had gotten comfortable after getting married and having children, as if I had forgotten that I once really battled with these ideas.

My desire for diversity in the culture and makeup of my church was confirmed as I read about John Piper's efforts for more inclusiveness within his congregation. Concerning music he wrote, "We continually attempt to define our musical center in corporate worship in such a way that it includes a range of ethnic expressions."[5]

Anthony Carter, author of *On Being Black and Reformed*, takes it further and says, "A theological perspective that fails to speak contextually to African-American life, whether orthodox or liberal, will not gain a hearing among people who have become skeptical of the establishment."[6]

It was comforting to be reminded by leaders whom I respect that it is okay to have a desire for diversity in music, activities, and the general environment. It is okay to think that, overall, the music, activities, and general environment should consider the *entire congregation*. Did you catch that? I'm not just saying music; it's the activities as well. As I've mentioned before, my church had wonderful events, but they were often geared toward one audience. If your church is truly seeking diversity (in any way), your activities must be diverse. This includes the activities for women. Doing brunches exclusively at a country club may not be extremely inviting for your black sister.[7]

That is only a small taste of what I had been thinking through, and I finally shared what I had been both thinking and praying about for nearly thirteen years (obviously off and on). And though I wasn't aware of it back in the early years of my church attendance, I was discovering what the Scriptures have to say about diversity. I was formulating a theology for diversity. What

DIVERSITY DISPLAYS A TRUE UNDERSTANDING OF THE GRACE OF GOD

began as a mere feeling of rejection had been transformed into something beautiful—a desire for diversity for the benefit of the church.

I will address the numerous benefits of diversity in the coming chapters, but one clear benefit must be mentioned here: by building into diverse relationships, we display the reconciliation and redemption of Christ to a world that is broken and divided. True unity is found first through being reconciled to God and then to each other. To walk in that unity arm in arm with people of every tribe and race is to declare to the world that Christ's blood is enough for the fight for racial reconciliation.

Additionally, diversity displays a true understanding of the grace of God. As Dr. Piper states, "Every true Christian, of every class and culture and race, is indwelt by the living Son of God who loved us and gave himself for us. . . . It is impossible to really believe and revel in that truth and yet mistreat a believer of a different race."[8] We cannot live redemptive lives and hate our neighbor. Diversity in relationships not only shows unity to the world but also builds in our own hearts a love for others. It is the same love that Christ has for all people.

The Bible addresses so clearly that God saves all people regardless of ethnicity and that the last days will be filled with all the nations (Romans 3:23–24; Revelation 5:9). It makes sense that somewhere in my heart I wanted to be a part of a church that displays this beauty *now*. God was working in me what I believe is clearly displayed through Scripture—diversity benefits the church, displays the last days, demonstrates the power of the gospel, and glorifies God.

I knew my longing wasn't sinful, as long as I wasn't discontented, so I hoped that God would bring diversity to my church.

And He did.

God did not answer that prayer and desire through a mass influx of varying ethnicities to the body of believers that I was a part of; He did answer in a most generous way: by giving me best friends.

CHAPTER 4
GOD'S PROVISION OF DIVERSITY

GOD WORKS IN MYSTERIOUS WAYS.

We've heard that saying, and it's true. God does work in ways that are often unexpected and unexplainable. That was the case with me in 2001. I had recently joined my church, and though I was thankful to be there, I continued to long for diversity.

Each Thursday evening I attended my church's campus-ministry night at the University of Tennessee. Through my attendance there, I started to get to know a few girls, but I hadn't built any deep relationships. There was one girl whom I had only slowly begun to know. We ended up together in a senior-level political science class and said hello from time to time, but we hadn't really interacted much beyond the occasional hello. Then one day she approached me and invited me to have dinner before the next campus meeting.

Amy and I met in a cafeteria on campus in the middle of all the dormitories. That particular cafeteria was a favorite among the students because it served Chick-fil-A—chicken sandwich, waffle fries, Icedream cone, yes, please. She had brought another young girl with her, which was a nice surprise. I didn't know Lillian's nationality at the time, but I knew she was Asian. As we sat together and enjoyed the meal, Amy suggested that we start meeting together regularly. She was an intern with the campus ministry, and part of her desire was to disciple me. I was happy to begin meeting because I was eager to have girlfriends.

We began meeting regularly, and it quickly became apparent that these were girls with whom I not only "clicked" but also would grow. We had small-group meetings every other Friday at the home of a family from church, and before heading to that home each week, we cooked a meal together. Actually, being the resident cook, I prepared spaghetti, and Amy and Lillian brought either bread or salad and sparkling grape juice. We then spent two hours laughing, crying, and praying together.

Friday nights became the most anticipated night of the week. Though we had two hours to talk, it was not long enough for three expressive and passionate women! For some reason, Amy often spoke first, prompted by the question, "What's on your heart, girl?" She would grin and then share something similar to what she had shared the week before. Then Lillian would talk, and by the time she was finished, her tender heart would give way and she would cry. I went last, and they always felt the need to encourage me to choose one thing to "work on" rather than ten.

We quickly became not just friends but the best of friends. Amy and I, in particular, spent more time with each other than any friends ought to. We were attached at the hip. Little did Amy and Lillian know that their friendships were a gift, not only because of the special relationships that developed but also because they fulfilled my desire for diversity.

Diversity doesn't mean "more of the same." Maybe that's obvious. But for me at that time, my longing for diversity was being fulfilled not because God had brought in more black people (though I would have been thrilled if that had been the case), but because He had united me with people who were unlike me. God knew my desire for diversity and graciously provided Lillian (Chinese) and Amy (white). Lillian grew up in the United States with Chinese missionary parents. Amy grew up outside of Chicago in a Christian home. And then there was me, a black girl from the South.

In order to fully grasp the significance of our friendship, you'll need to sit back and get to know them a little. They were two special girlfriends who played pivotal roles in my Christian development. We were also very different. Each of us had incredibly varied stories and upbringings. It's these differences that truly made our friendship special.

MEET AMY

Amy grew up in Highland, Indiana, a small but crowded white, blue-collar, working-class town in northwest Indiana near Chicago. Right near Highland is Gary, Indiana, a primarily black city, also just outside Chicago, often noted for crime and as the hometown of The Jackson 5 (the childhood singing group of Michael Jackson and his siblings). Amy's northern characteristics would come out most in her speech. "I need a pop," she might say. *Pop, what's a pop? You mean you want a Coke, right?* It didn't take too much observation to see that she and I were very different. But I think what set us apart most was her faith.

She was raised in a wonderful Christian home. She was also the oldest of five kids. Her dad was a carpenter until she was a teenager, at which time he became a self-made architect. Her mom was a stay-at-home mother and, as Amy says, "raised us with very little rules, lots of prayer, and much grace and kindness." This is where Amy and I have similar experiences. I remember my mother being down on the floor every night praying for what seemed (to a child) like hours, though it was probably only twenty or thirty minutes. My sisters and I were also seemingly rule-less. Amy's dad worked a lot, but when he was home, she says, "he showed a passion for my mom, evangelism, and anyone in need."

I remember Amy sharing a story about her father. He was at a parade and saw a woman whom he knew was not a Christian, and immediately he began to proclaim Christ to her. Her stories always left me wide-eyed and jaw-dropped. I had seen passion for sports and even social issues but not for Christ. That was new to me. Amy grew up in an intensely passionate home—not passionate in terms of communication or general emotions but passionate about Christ. Apart from that, they were actually rather reserved.

That is where Amy and I were most different. I grew up in a passionate family also, but we were passionate communicators. We weren't afraid to share what we thought. We were okay with conflict. There wasn't much guessing required as to how each of us felt about things. Amy, on the other hand, was outgoing and very warm but reserved about her personal life. I believe this was partly because of her upbringing. But once we got to know each other, we were inseparable. She reflects on her home life:

Our home life was peaceful (other than typical brother-sister fights) and served as the headquarters for all the neighborhood kids. There were constantly people at our house. For a while we even had someone live with us—a lady my mom had met at an abortion clinic. My mom tried to get in gentle conversations with women entering the clinic in hopes of persuading them to leave. The only season of real strife I recall was when I was a young teenager and began to chafe under my dad's authority. I hated the (reasonable) curfew he gave me and that I wasn't allowed to see all the movies my friends could. I fought with him a lot during this time and couldn't be reasoned with. I'm thankful that God changed my heart toward my dad just a few months before he died of a stroke. I was sixteen years old. It was such a drastic change in me that I finally got serious about my faith. During that trial I experienced a radical love for Jesus that I'd never had to that degree before. I was encountering God every day in a powerful and new way.

Amy and I shared the grief of losing our fathers at young ages. My father passed away when I was nineteen years old. As young women in college trying to find our way into adulthood, Amy and I missed our fathers. We leaned on each other often and were "adopted" by our small group leaders.

Although Amy grew up in the suburbs, and many of her friends were white, she did have the opportunity to attend a diverse Christian school through the eighth grade. She remembers it as a wonderful experience:

> It felt very normal at the time, but now I look back and realize how different it could have been if I'd attended the public elementary and middle school in my town. I wouldn't have seen how normal friendships can be between races, because it wouldn't have been part of my experience. When I entered public high school, the experience was different in that it was mostly white, but my opinions on race were already cemented at that point. It was clear to me that all races are equal before God and can have unique cultural differences that are interesting and fun to learn about and experience rather than something to be feared. I don't believe I was influenced negatively by living near Gary. I always saw Gary as having a poverty and

crime problem rather than a race problem.

Amy reflected the environment she was raised in. She was unassuming and kind, incredibly gracious toward those who were different from her (in belief and practice). She and I quickly became the best of friends, although there was little at all about our backgrounds to unite us.

Lillian had a similar upbringing as Amy in that she also grew up in a Christian home, but like me, she was from the South.

MEET LILLIAN

Lillian grew up in Nashville, Tennessee, approximately three hours from where I was raised. Her father was a full-time pastor and worked for the Sunday School Board of the Southern Baptist Convention, now LifeWay Christian Resources. Many of her childhood memories are of being in church on Sundays, both morning and evening, as well as Wednesday nights and sometimes Saturdays. This seems to be the unique experience of a pastor's kid. I can't imagine being at church that much as a child! I think I would have rebelled. I would have been the kid sneaking out to "use the bathroom," encouraging other kids to do the same, and playing in a secret spot. Lillian's dad was a pastor of a Chinese church that was hosted in a predominantly white Baptist church. Because of her poor Chinese language skills, Lillian and her two sisters attended another church they called "American church." Lillian recalls her upbringing:

My parents were unlike most other typical Chinese parents. Most of my Chinese friends had very high expectations placed on them from their parents to succeed academically as well as to participate and excel in extracurricular subjects. My parents did not send us to music classes, Chinese lessons, or extracurricular activities. My parents encouraged and expected us to do well in school, but as long as we worked hard and put forth our best efforts, they were pleased. We were the first generation in our family to grow up in America. I suppose my parents' experiences of being raised in Hong Kong and by unbelievers led them to use different parenting practices with us. My mother played piano and taught all of my siblings and me. That went on until we all outwardly complained about the lessons. So my mother one day just asked us if we wanted to continue. Of course, we said no, and she didn't force it on us. We each regret the decision to this day! But this is just a small example of how my parents never pushed us to do anything outside of school.

Though Lillian's parents didn't push her in school, she was pulled to church as a young child. Her parents were devoted to their church and to the community. She recalls her church life:

We went to church three days a week, which led us as young children to perceive our parents as strict. Yet as we grew older, we could see that it was the love of Christ that compelled them to be at church so much and their desire to show God's love to us by being gracious and not strict. One thing pressed in my mind, besides spending entire Sundays at church, is how my parents prayed and pursued the lost. My mother was always praying. In the mornings I would find her sitting on her neatly made bed, Bible in her lap, blanket across her shoulders, head bowed in her hands. And my father always opened our home to people, whether new visitors at the Chinese church coming for meals, counseling, or questions about the Bible, or the young girl who came from China with no job or English skills and lived with us for two years. Those specific memories fill my childhood and remind me of my parents' love for God.

Lillian and I shared experiences of growing up in the South in predominately white cities, which were similar in that our identities were confused by our environment. Though we both experienced racism while growing up, Lillian never spoke of it. I, on the other hand, did but not often. The major difference between us was that she didn't feel different unless someone pointed it out to her. I felt different even when no one said much to me about being different. My feelings were definitely elevated by comments, but I also realized those feelings are part of being human. Lillian explains her experience of growing up in a predominantly white environment:

I was almost always the minority in my circle of friends—there were rarely any Hispanic, African-Americans, or Latin Americans in my group. In all my elementary school pictures, you could easily spot me. I was always at the end of the row—a bowl haircut and the tallest one. A perfect formula to be set apart from other kids and to be made fun of. Check, check, and check! But I do believe that weird time in elementary and middle school is what the Lord used to save me at that young age. Ironically, because I was always immersed in a predominately white environment, I never even really felt Chinese. Because I dressed, acted, and talked like everyone else, I felt different only when I was made fun of or ridiculed for being Chinese, which really only started in middle school. I went to a magnet high school that purposely had certain ratios of varying ethnic groups. So this was the first time I was exposed to lots of people from different countries. Caucasians were probably the minority in that school. Though, in a sense, it was forced integration, we didn't see it that way. We were all friends; it was an awesome experience.

I share their stories to give you a taste of just how different we three are. We came together with all of our differences (not just in ethnicity), and I think it was because of those things—nurtured by communication and the Lord—that allowed us to grow into the women we are today.

DIFFERENT AS A GIFT

As it relates to race, I often hear people say things like, "I don't see color; we are all the same," or, "Why do we have to talk about race when we are all the same?" Here's the thing: you do see color. Unless you are truly color blind, you see color. And this is a good thing! I understand that such statements are said with good intentions, but what might be more accurate is to say that you don't immediately equate characteristics and stereotypes to a color. That's obviously also a good thing. But diversity in and of itself also is a good thing, and unfortunately differences aren't always celebrated in others.

I think part of this resistance to acknowledge or accept differences is rooted in a fear to insult or offend. Our country's history definitely lends itself to this tension. And of course there are truly offensive ways to recognize differences. I'm not advocating that people walk around pointing out the obvious color difference or unique cultural clothing of others. That's not what I mean. Amy, Lillian, and I got to know each other deeply. We became friends. Our differences didn't pull us farther from each other; rather, they united us. God employed our differences for our benefit and mutual encouragement, which I'll be discussing further in chapter 6.

The good news is that we don't have to pretend to be color blind. I don't think that's what God intended for us to do when He created the world with all of its variety and said it was good. As image bearers of God, we can be comfortable that God created us (and those of different ethnicities) uniquely, which is good. We can celebrate and embrace our differences. We should celebrate our difference because we are made in the image of God.

IMAGO DEI

As God's image bearers we are all equal. We are equal in dignity and worth. We are created equally in His image. We are also fallen equally (Romans 3:23). Genesis 1:26 explains that God created man in His image. Of all God's creation, we are the only ones created in His very image; we have dominion over the rest (Genesis 1:28). It is a profound mystery (God is spirit, so we do not bear His physical image, John 4:24) and yet a great privilege. Understanding our equality as image bearers changes everything we think about our human relationships.

As image bearers we should view others as God views us. One way the Lord identifies us, and I'd argue, the most important, is that either we are in Christ or we are not. C. S. Lewis said it best when he wrote:

There are no ordinary people. You have never talked to a mere mortal. Nations, cultures, arts, civilizations—these are mortal, and their life is to ours as the life of a gnat. But it is immortals whom we joke with,

work with, marry, snub and exploit—immortal horrors or everlasting splendours. This does not mean
that we are to be perpetually solemn. We must play.
But our merriment must be of that kind (and it is, in
fact, the merriest kind) which exists between people
who have, from the outset, taken each other seriously
—no flippancy, no superiority, no presumption.[1]

We are not merely individuals walking out our faith
alone. We are a part of humanity, each one of us heading
toward heaven or hell. We want to be mindful as we interact
with others that though the here and now may feel and seem
incredibly permanent, it is not. This doesn't mean that we
view people as projects. That isn't love. But out of love we
remember that those of us in Christ are witnesses. We want
to share the gospel and be a light in a darkened world. It's the
greatest news we've ever heard. We don't want to keep it to
ourselves.

And yet we have a barrier that we must overcome, and
that is understanding racial identities and what the Bible says
about them.

THE BIBLE AND RACE

There possibly isn't a more complex yet important topic
as race as it relates to the Word of God and the church. To
understand our differences and why they are good, we must
first understand our origin. Because of the sin of partiality
and pride, it is problematic for some to truly believe the idea

of racial equality. But this equality isn't a man-made, modern, social justice theory. We aren't arguing for something unjust. Rather, the equality of people originated from God.

J. Daniel Hays wrote a compelling book, *From Every People and Nation*, addressing the biblical theology of race. In it he explores the origins of race and ethnicity, looking at current-day definitions, stereotypes, and poor biblical interpretation; reevaluating the concepts; and expounding Scripture. For him, and for us, understanding race begins with understanding Adam, the first man. He writes:

> The Bible does not begin with the creation of a special race of people. When the first human is introduced into the story he is simply called 'ādām, which means "humankind." . . . Their "race" is not identifiable; they are neither Negroid nor Caucasian, nor even Semitic. They become the mother and father of all peoples. The division of humankind into peoples and races is not even mentioned until Genesis 10.[2]

Racially generic Adam represents all of humankind made in the *imago Dei* (image of God). We are *all* made in God's image, but what does that mean? I attempted to share thoughts about that in the section above, but scholars have debated what it means to be made in the image of God. According to Hays, it has been widely accepted to mean that humans share God's mental and spiritual faculties though certainly to a *far* lesser degree.[3] We are unique in God's creation, able to rule over animals and the earth; we have souls; and we are able to commune with God. We are made for fellowship, reflecting the triune God.

Psalm 8 proclaims: "O Lord, our Lord, how majestic is your name in all the earth! You have set your glory above the heavens. . . . What is man that you are mindful of him, and the son of man that you care for him? Yet you have made him a little lower than the heavenly beings and crowned him with glory and honor" (vv. 1, 4–5). God has given each of us dominion over the works of His hands, equally. God is mindful of each person He creates, equally. Understanding our equality before the Lord and the origins of creation should be enough to break the barriers of racial strife. But perhaps part of our confusion is derived from a misinterpretation of Genesis 9:1–27 and the so-called curse of Ham.

Hays describes this misinterpretation as one of the "most damaging misinterpretations of Scripture on the subject of race," and understandably so. It's this interpretation that slave owners and segregationists used to justify slavery.

So what happened? Genesis states that the people of the whole earth were dispersed from Shem, Ham, and Japheth, the sons of Noah. Ham was the father of Canaan; that's important to state upfront. One night Noah became drunk and lay naked and uncovered in his tent. The youngest of the brothers, Ham, saw his father and then grabbed his brothers Japheth and Shem to see. When the other brothers came, they covered Noah. Upon awakening, Noah, humiliated by the series of events, cursed Canaan, the son of Ham, stating that Canaan would be "a servant of servants shall he be to his brothers" (v. 25). The curse fell on Canaan alone and not on all of Ham's sons. Unfortunately, the curse has been misapplied to all of Ham's descendants rather than just to Canaan.

The significance of the events comes in Genesis 10 when we learn that Ham's descendants are the Cushites, who are linked geographically to Africa. Throughout history, Christians have justified slavery by citing the so-called curse of Ham as proof that black Africans were destined and designated for such a station in life. This misinterpretation infiltrated the American South, and after the Civil War, it was used heavily within the church. Hays again writes:

> After the American Civil War, the "curse of Ham" was used by white clergymen to fight the notion of racial equality and the rights that would accompany such equality (voting, education, etc.). Richard Rivers, for example, editor of the Louisville *Central Methodist*, argued in an 1889 editorial for the popular view that, so long as the two races must live together on American soil, the Black man "must occupy the position of inferiority," and that "Ham must be subservient to Japheth."[4]

Japheth's descendants were coastland people, and they settled in Europe and Asia Minor and are thus interpreted as being racially white. The misinterpretation of Genesis, though not widely accepted now, continues to be reprinted in commentaries even today. Again, the curse has been misapplied to all of Ham's descendants rather than just to Canaan. What is also interesting—and further undermines the modern "curse of Ham" application—is that the Canaanites are ethnically most similar to the Israelites.[5]

DOES RACE EVEN EXIST?

Before I move on, I'd like to note that for some, the concept of race not only doesn't appear in the Bible, but it is actually fabricated. In other words, the origins of race are not rooted in Scripture but in a sociological construct. Senior pastor of First Baptist Church of Grand Cayman and author Thabiti Anyabwile has taken up the cause to rid the world of the term *race*, and he argues that the word *race* was developed for four reasons: society, the fall of man (which we will look at), psychology, and interaction with people (he would say blacks helped define "whiteness" for whites, and whites helped define "blackness" for blacks).[6] His basic premise is that because of our origin (all created in the image of God with Adam as our representative), we are one mankind with varying tongues, nations, tribes, families, and skin color, but there is little to nothing genetically or biologically that makes us different races (or species). We are all the same race (i.e., species). In his view it would be more accurate for us to identify one another by our ethnicities, which is in the Bible.

In a recent interview I conducted with Pastor Anyabwile, which is available in its entirety in the appendix, he elaborates on this point:

When we read the Bible, one useful question to ask ourselves is: What story is the Bible telling me about the origin of humanity and its diversity? When we ask that question, we see several things. First, Eve is "the mother of all the living" (Genesis 3:20 NIV). Second, several generations later, the human line is narrowed again to one family, that of Noah and his sons (Genesis 6–9). All the families of the earth are descended from Noah's three sons and their wives (Genesis 10). "From these the nations spread out over the earth after the flood" (v. 32 NIV). These "nations" are not national city-states, but "clans and languages, in their territories." In other words, these are large kinship and language groups. The story the Bible tells is one of *continuity*, not discontinuity, which "race" at least implies. So you get the pronouncement of Acts 17:26—"From one man he made every nation of men, that they should inhabit the whole earth" (NIV).

This is the way the Bible speaks of our common ancestry and of the ethnic diversity we seek. It's a diversity within the same species, if you will. In fact, genetic science has proven that there is no subspecies in mankind. There's not enough genetic variance to meet the tests of science.

Think of the grief and despair that would have been avoided had we always operated under these convictions. Nonetheless, this is not widely accepted or understood at the moment, and part of that (if not all) is due to the fall of man.

SIN CORRUPTS AND DIVIDES

Some might argue that God's design was never for man to be diverse, at least not in speech and culture, which is why in Genesis He scattered the people, causing confusion. God's original design and creation were perfect. But it wasn't culture that caused the great divide among men—it was sin.

In the beginning, we know that God created man and woman in His image (Genesis 1:27). Sin came into the world and instantaneously Adam and Eve were at odds with each other. She would want to rule over her husband, and her husband over her; childbirth would be difficult; work would become a hardship; and eventually man would die and return to the ground that was once perfect but had become part of the fall (Genesis 3:16–19).

But why did these curses have to happen? Adam and Eve chose to ignore God's instruction and instead go their own way, enticed by the lie of the Serpent, and they fell. In much the same way, we look to Genesis 11 and find the whole earth speaking one language and unified in a quest to build a tower. No problems with that, but their construction was actually an effort to make a name for themselves and establish their independence from God. The builders' goal was contrary to the desires of God; they did not want to be dispersed over the face of the earth, so they set out to build their Tower of Babel (Genesis 1:22, 28; 9:1, 7; 11:4).

So what did God do? He punished them and scattered

the people, confusing their language, and dispersing them "over the face of all the earth" (Genesis 11:8). The confusion of languages wasn't the actual punishment. No, God was preventing people from becoming powerful, proud, and self-sufficient. God knew that man's sinful heart and desire for praise and glory would be too great of a temptation, and therefore He would need to confuse the language (11:7).

But this language confusion was also part of God's redemption story. He sent Christ to die for every tongue and nation, and all tribes will be present on the last day (speaking their native tongue), praising God with one voice (Romans 1:16; Revelation 7:9). These differences won't go away on the last day. God will create a new heaven and a new earth, and all will be perfected—and languages and tribes will remain intact, perfectly united.

DIFFERENCES DIVIDE

Unfortunately, our differences often divide rather than unite us. Our confusion has turned into hate and discrimination on all sides from every tribe. We see that these are deep-rooted issues that have been taught for centuries in our churches and throughout society. God gives us a picture of His view of racism when Moses is confronted by Miriam and Aaron for his marrying a Cushite (Ethiopian) woman (Numbers 12:1). The Lord appeared before them, rebuked Miriam, and then caused her skin to turn "leprous, like snow" (v. 10). This is why it's so important that we understand our origins and the history of our nation. Getting this right, as right as we can with our finite minds, is obviously important to God too. No one is exempt from the temptation of pride and arrogance toward their neighbor.

Amy recalls how our differences, though not often thought of as we met together all those years, helped her to realize that racism still exists:

> I just saw us as three girls getting to know each other—all from different places with different experiences—but that's how it is with anyone you're getting to know, since there will always be unique things about people, even if you do happen to be from the same place and have the same skin color. I have learned from Trillia the very real and ongoing racism that is still alive and present in many hearts. She has told me stories of times when she has been the object of racism. I wouldn't even know that many of these things still happen if it weren't for her. It's been very eye-opening.

I never expected Amy to understand the racism that I had experienced in the South. But as we got to know each other, she learned and began to carry my burden. My burden became her burden. That is one of the beauties of our friendship—we began to carry burdens that we would not and could not fully relate to. The result is that this ultimately equipped us to serve others beyond our small sphere. We saw this played out mostly in evangelism. All three of us girls had a heart for other people, and I believe our unique bond and understanding of others helped us be uninhibited by ethnicity or culture when attempting to reach the lost.

We weren't three girls just trying to relate as merely white, black, and Chinese. We were women drawn to each other because of the grace of God. Each of us shared Lillian's sentiment: "I know our differing ethnicities were not the reason that I was drawn to each of you as friends. I was drawn to you both because of your love for God and how you each spurred me on to love Him. And you were and are super fun gals!" But we were also distinctly different and celebrated those differences. Our nickname ("Black, White, and Chinese"—not exactly unique!) reflected that we didn't forget that God made us in His image but different. We loved it. Differences can divide, but they don't have to; they don't need to.

Yet we had a bond that surpassed any culture or ethnicity. Our bond was blood bought. We were bound together in Christ, by Christ, as sisters. Our friendship not only brought the diversity I longed for; it redefined what it meant to be a sister.

CHAPTER 5
DIFFERENT BUT THE SAME

BLACK, WHITE, CHINESE—Amy, Lillian, and I didn't set out to meet because we were ethnically diverse. That didn't cross our minds at first. We did, however, celebrate our differences as we continued to grow in our friendships. These differences proved to be a benefit to our growth in godliness, which we will explore further in chapter 6. Our friendship was a sweet display to the world of the gospel. But we were united by the fact that in God's family, we are the same.

HIS IMAGE

The term *sister*, commonly pronounced *sis-ta*, often refers to black women. It's derived from the traditional black-church pattern of referring to female members of the church family as "sista."[1] When I was in college, there weren't a lot of "sistas" in my church, but I found a new sisterhood with Amy and Lillian. We were sisters in Christ—perhaps the most intimate and meaningful sisterhood.

When the world talks about racial reconciliation, the emphasis is on getting along. The focus for this racial reconciliation is rooted in a desire for the races to relate and merely like one another. While I believe people genuinely desire to love and accept one another, God's Word takes it a step further and is much more meaningful. As Christians, we aren't merely meant to get along. We aren't merely to love—we are to love as if we are blood-related sisters and brothers.

When God created the world, He did not distinguish just some to be made in His image. Every person, all ethnicities, are made in the image of God (Genesis 1:27). You probably know this by now, as I continue to mention it. In Acts 17 Paul addresses the Areopagus, saying, "He made from one man *every nation* of mankind to live on all the face of the earth" (v. 26, emphasis mine). The implications are astounding! Think about it: you and I are made in the very image of God. When Amy, Lillian, and I met together, we met as image bearers of the Creator of the universe—equally.

As John Piper once said, "In determining the significance of who you are, being a person in the image of God compares to ethnic distinctives the way the noonday sun compares to a candlestick."[2]

Piper's imagery of the noonday sun, bright and high and lifted up, compared to a measly candlestick gives us a great picture of how insignificant (though still important) our differences are. The significance of our being made in the *imago Dei* renders our differences in ethnicity nearly trivial. The most important aspect of our ethnicity is to remember that it was created by God. So we are equal in creation and equal in image bearing. It truly is amazing. Like the psalmist, we cry out, "What is man that you are mindful of him, and the son of man that you care for him? Yet you have made him a little lower than the heavenly beings and crowned him with glory and honor" (Psalm 8:4–5).

But I believe it gets even sweeter than this.

NEW SISTERHOOD

We are made in His image, and we are brought into a special family—a special relationship designated only for born-again Christians (John 3:5; 1 Peter 1:3). Upon believing, we are ushered into a new family and counted as children of God (John 1:12–13). John makes clear that the new birth is not of man but of God. We are accepted into God's family regardless of our supposed good works and our ethnicity, which is yet another reminder that there is no distinction between ethnicities in the kingdom of God. There is one family, and all are welcomed because of the blood of Christ shed on our behalf. Once we've placed our faith and trust in Jesus, we are all counted as God's children.

It may be difficult for some to imagine a family that is functioning well—united and loving. You might come from a broken family, a family riddled with hardship, or no family at all. Some of you may not be speaking to a member of your family. So when I write with great enthusiasm about family and how we are sisters and brothers in Christ, it might seem discouraging or even impossible. Hard circumstances can skew our vision of the good things God has. That is what makes the family of God so special. There is a camaraderie and a love for one another that is rooted in the blood of Christ. It is unique.

Jesus affirmed the importance of the new family when He addressed the people while His mother and brothers stood outside. As they waited for Him, He declared, "'Who is my mother, and who are my brothers?' And stretching out his hand toward his disciples, he said, 'Here are my mother and my brothers! For whoever does the will of my Father in heaven is my brother and sister and mother'" (Matthew 12:48–50).

Jesus isn't making a statement that our biological families are no longer important. Rather He is stating that following Him is far greater. He takes priority, and so does His kingdom—so much so that those who follow Him He counts as His brother and sister and mother—His family.

Don't misunderstand. I am not saying we should ditch our families for our brothers and sisters in Christ. I have two biological sisters, who are two of my best friends, and one deceased. God graciously placed me into a blood family, and we love each other dearly. The point is that the kingdom family is important and unique. It's so important that Jesus gave His life for this family and now allows us the privilege of being His brothers and sisters. Amazing!

Our spiritual family reaches back generations. We are "children of God, and if children, then heirs—heirs of God and fellow heirs with Christ" (Romans 8:16–17). All generations past and those yet to be seen are a part of this family.

And as heirs, all the promises of God are equally ours in this family. We are so much a part of God's family that He even disciplines us, treating and shaping us as good parents do for their children. Without discipline, we are "illegitimate children and not sons" (Hebrews 12:8).

Amy and Lillian aren't merely my friends; they are my sisters. We are each children of God (1 John 3:1). As Christians, we are also a part of one body. In God's creativity He gives the church body varying gifts, talents, colors, and personalities. We are all called to different functions in this one body; nevertheless, it is *one* body (Romans 12:4–5). John Piper explains, "All believers in Jesus Christ, of every ethnic group, are united to each other, not only in a common humanity in the image of God, but even more, as brothers and sisters in Christ and members of the same body."[3]

His words are yet another reminder of good news. God doesn't choose His children because of how they look. He doesn't say you must be tall, light-skinned, blonde, or green-eyed to be part of His family. It gets better: you don't need to have perfect obedience to be accepted into His family either. Yep—the gospel doesn't require our good works. To be a child of God requires one thing—Christ—and when we place our faith in Him, we are all counted as equal children. He's got a colorful family, and therefore so do we. Russell Moore puts it like this in his book *Adopted for Life*:

> Our adoption means . . . that we find a different kind of unity. In Christ, we find Christ. We don't have our

old identities based on race or class or life situation. The Spirit drives us from Babel to Pentecost, which is why "the works of the flesh" Paul warns about include "enmity, strife, jealousy." . . . When we find our identity anywhere other than Christ, our churches will be made up of warring partisans rather than loving siblings. . . .

What would it mean, though, if we took the radical notion of being brothers and sisters seriously? What would happen if your church saw an elderly woman no one would ever confuse with "cool" on her knees at the front of the church praying with a body-pierced fifteen-year-old anorexic girl? What would happen if your church saw a white millionaire corporate vice president being mentored by a Latino minimum wage-earning janitor because both know the janitor is more mature in the things of Christ?[4]

Yes. What if we took this notion seriously?

Our friendships would radically change. Our interactions with others would radically change. Why? Because we'd see each other as equally sinful, equally in need of grace, and equally redeemed. We'd have a very different view of one another.

So am I thinking rightly? My Chinese and white girlfriends are my sisters? Yes, they are. We are united in Christ —the only thing that matters—and we can function as sisters, which we have done.

Thinking about the special relationship I had with my biological sisters, I am reminded of times growing up when we would share secrets, argue, play with imaginary friends, and talk about boys. (I had an imaginary boyfriend named Michael; he was biracial.) My sisters and I would climb in bed together on Christmas Eve and wake up at 5:00 a.m. to open presents. We kept up that tradition through our teenage years. Even now I speak with one or both of them each week, the youngest one close to every day.

That same sisterly camaraderie reflects my relationship with Amy and Lillian.

We were much older when we became close, so we didn't play with imaginary friends, but we sure did dream of future plans of marriage, children, or even where we'd live. We knew everything about one another, so there were plenty of times for secret sharing. Amy and I went swing dancing with a group from church and then returned to the basement of the family's home in which she was living and stayed up until 5:00 a.m. talking. Till this day I can't figure out how we functioned the next day. Now, married with children, I can hardly stay up past 10:00 p.m.

I just recently called Amy to share an encouraging secret. I'd tell you, but it's our little secret. That's the beauty of close friends. And what girl doesn't talk about boys? We were all engaged at the same time and married within months of each other. Each of us was in the others' weddings as bridesmaids. Boys, fears, the wedding night, and you name it were hot topics during those days.

We were sisters. We *are* sisters.

We were incredibly different in nearly every way, yet we found commonality and unity in Christ. And not only commonality and unity, but in the sight of God we are literally counted as equal image bearers, His children, in the household of God. We are the same. It is because of this sameness that diversity is beautiful and possible in Christ.

My friends were equally affected by our sisterhood, though Amy would say she never considered the theology of covenant relationships within the church. Amy recalls:

> I didn't think of us as sisters but did feel we had a very special, unique friendship. I learned so much from you guys, probably *because* we all came from different families, places, perspectives, etc. Also, even though I didn't think in terms of family per se, I was actually more open with you guys in some ways than I was with my sisters.

And Lillian expresses her thoughts: "Because of our union together in Christ Jesus, yes, I did consider us sisters! And that goes beyond blood and skin. Our hearts were beginning to be sewn together through our times of rich fellowship and sharing hardships and encouragement."

Our friendship had an effect on how I viewed my relationships with my close friends and also on how I viewed the relationships between the members of my church. The Word addresses the church, not in terms of best friends but as members of God's family. Even people I've never spoken with are like my family in the eyes of God.

As we begin to view members of our churches as members of God's family and thus as members of our family, our prejudices begin to crumble. Racial reconciliation is not only possible; it's a must because we are the very family of God. That's astounding.

We are created equally. When Christ calls us to Himself, He does not look at who we are in terms of ethnicity, nor does He call us because of who we are in any other way except that we are dead and in need of new life. We are equally saved. As a result, our churches should be the most gracious environments on the planet. More than any other place, the church should be more open to and excited about having people unlike themselves. This gracious environment must begin in our hearts. We have to look to Jesus and ask for grace to emulate His grace. All this equality should transform the way we interact with others, including our pursuit of deep and

UNDERSTANDING THE FAMILY OF GOD IS YET ANOTHER WEAPON AGAINST RACIAL INTOLERANCE IN THE CHURCH. AS WE RECOGNIZE, ACCEPT, AND EMBRACE OUR NEW FAMILY, THE WALLS OF HOSTILITY WILL CRUMBLE.

meaningful friendships and how we view members of the body.

Although Amy wouldn't have equated the church body with family, she grew up in an environment in which her family implemented such characteristics through their open-door policy, constantly hosting guests. Amy shares:

> I have always felt that the family of God was very important. Growing up, this was reinforced by our never missing church unless we were terribly sick and being very involved in church events and with the lives of our church family. I was raised surrounded with examples of people being family to each other in the church, so even though my accountability experience with Lillian and Trillia was awesome, I don't think it changed my perception of church being like family.

Understanding the family of God is yet another weapon against racial intolerance in the church. As we recognize, accept, and embrace our new family, the walls of hostility will crumble. Our friendships were unique because we were three girls from different backgrounds and ethnicities. Only in the family of God can three people so distinctly different be the same (equal in creation and redemption) and counted as sisters in a new family. Lillian captures this thought as she reflects on our friendships:

Our friendships were unique, and I suppose I did not realize really how special they were at the time. As time passed and we all entered new seasons in life, only then did I see what God had done in our hearts over the years. It helped me also to see that when God gave us Christ and that we the church are His bride, I became a part of something very big. When I later became a member of our church, I realized how God was knitting our hearts together in our friendships. And through our friendships, over time, I began to see just how vital it was for me to be part of a church body and that I was benefiting from what God intends His church to be. We were bound together in Christ as blood sisters would be. We were in the family of Christ, sewn together as believers and enjoying sweet fellowship with Jesus and with one another!

Understanding the family of God is yet another weapon against racial intolerance in the church. As we recognize, accept, and embrace our new family, the walls of hostility will crumble. We are indeed different because God's creation is unique, but we are much more the same than we are different. At the core of who we are as created beings, thought of before the creation of the world, knit together in our mother's womb, made in the image of God, and redeemed by the blood of the cross, we are the same. We are the same! Sin and perhaps ignorance distorts this beautiful picture of sameness and makes our differences the Enemy's doing rather than part of God's good creation. We no longer have to allow sin and ignorance to reign. My friends and I made a decision to embrace our differences. We all can, because of the renewing work of the Spirit, make that same choice.

Similar to those in any family, Lillian, Amy, and I were different from one another. But as we've seen, in God's economy we were the same. The things that make us unique are gifts from God, and He uses them mightily in our growth in godliness.

CHAPTER 6
GROWING TOGETHER IN CHRIST

IN THINKING ABOUT DIVERSITY and people, we've already seen that God designed the world and all that is in it, so we know that diversity is really God's good idea. But, unfortunately, the word *diversity* has some baggage. I believe that in recent years this is, in part, due to affirmative action. The beauty of diversity has become a topic for political and social arguments. Maybe, for you, hearing the word *diversity* calls to mind diversity training meetings or quotas. But diversity, when we think in terms of God's creativity, is beautiful and beneficial for the church.

Diversity in the church isn't about quotas or filling a gap but about serving and loving others. We will explore this further later, but for now I want to share more about my friendships with Amy and Lillian and how God used our differences and diversity to mold us into the women we are today.

As we saw in chapter 5, Amy, Lillian, and I are different but ultimately the same; we are sisters in Christ. This bond set our relationships apart. We are united in mission and united by the blood of Christ. But there is no mistaking the fact that we are incredibly diverse. Our differences are at times strikingly apparent. Perhaps the most obvious is our skin color: brown, tan, white. But our differences are found in personality and gifting as well, and we have benefited greatly from it.

And why wouldn't we? The body isn't meant to be a monolithic homogenous gathering of people. Imagine it for a moment: every single person the exact same. God never intended it to be that way. I love the way Paul describes the church in 1 Corinthians 12:12–26: the body is made up of many varying parts and each part is needed for the whole body to function properly. We can't all be eyes or ears; we also need feet and hands and legs. Whatever you think might be the least significant part of your body, let's say a blood cell, is the very thing that keeps you alive.

Paul uses body parts as a metaphor to show the need for Christians to utilize the gifts God bestows on them upon conversion for the benefit of others. There is one thing that is clear to me in this passage: diversity of gifts and people are important for the edification of the body. Paul was directing his words to the Corinthians, urging them to use their gifts not for selfish gain or disorderly conduct but for the benefit of the whole body, and he stresses the importance of all members and each gift. He also calls for unity within the diversity of the gifts. We see this when, in verse 20, he says that though there are many parts (diversity), there is one body (unity).

Once again, God is directing our attention to the benefits of diversity. Though Paul does not directly identify various ethnic groups as he discusses the many parts, I argue that he doesn't exclude it either. He says, "For in one Spirit we were all baptized into one body—Jews or Greeks, slaves or free—and all were made to drink of one Spirit" (v. 13). We all have the same Spirit, and we are all—slave or free, Jew or Greek—useful for the church.

Amy, Lillian, and I have reflected on how our differences encouraged our faith in various ways. Amy is a woman of prayer. Lillian writes about her:

> I remember very specifically how Amy would pray and ask God for things. She would pray for big things and then also little things, such as a guitar. And, regardless of the magnitude of her request, all the while she prayed with lots of faith in God. And she actually was given a guitar soon after she prayed for one! That example of faith stirred in me a desire to pray like that—trusting and believing in a God who is sovereign and loves me because of Jesus Christ.

Amy learned to persevere in tough situations through watching me walk through various trials:

> When things weren't going well, Trillia fought to gain her strength in the Lord. I don't think I've learned this to the point of owning it, but I've definitely seen

her example of how to fight hard when I'm struggling. I've also learned to persevere in conflict and be willing to talk about problems as they arise rather than run from them (as is my tendency).

Lillian has been a great example of compassion. She oozed love from her pores. Tears would fall from her eyes as each of us girls would share our joys or sorrows. She was a walking, talking example of weeping with those who weep and rejoicing with those who rejoice (Romans 12:15).

Amy lives and walks by grace. I would not know and love the real good news of God's grace for sinners without the continual reminders I received from Amy. "For by grace you have been saved," she would proclaim boldly (see Ephesians 2:4–9) as she made decisions submitted to the Lord but absent of the fear of condemnation.

These little encouragements only scratch the surface of how we each benefited from one another. Obviously it is the Lord who transforms people to His likeness, but there was significant grace given to us because of our relationships. God in His kindness allowed us to develop meaningful relationships with one another, resulting in mutual encouragement.

GETTING PRACTICAL

In our culture, diversity gets celebrated each February. Schoolteachers pin up the faces of American black heroes such as Martin Luther King Jr., Rosa Parks, Booker T. Washington, and Thurgood Marshall. Churches break out old

Negro spirituals and host black pastors to preach. Black History Month provides a wonderful time for celebration and reflection.

But if we are truly going to build diversity within our churches, it must be more than once a year, and it must start outside the four walls of the church building. What I mean is, diversity isn't something we hope God will bring to our churches apart from our own investment outside of those four walls.

God provided me with a unique opportunity to celebrate diversity when I was a campus intern for my church. I was twenty-two when I began doing outreach and evangelism with my church's college ministry. When I began knocking on dorm room doors at the University of Tennessee, I was filled with excitement and anticipation. I thought to myself, *Who will reject me? Who will come to know Christ this year? What will I say when the door opens?* If no one opened the door, I would simply slide an invitation to our ministry kickoff under the door.

One of the girls I invited, Liz, came to a ministry kickoff. She was white, wore cowboy boots, listened to bluegrass, and was from Oregon. I was black and wore casual business attire. (Although I was doing campus ministry, at times I could be formal and businesslike. I might as well have had a briefcase.) I listened to jazz and liked to think I was from New York City. (I'm from Tennessee.)

As we got to know each other, we playfully ridiculed each other for our differences. We were polar opposites in so many ways. But in time she bought me a bluegrass CD, and I had her over for a black Southern-style Thanksgiving dinner (yes, it's different—a little collard greens and giblet gravy, just to name a few items).

She and I became the best of friends. We were different, but we were kindred spirits at the time. Why? Because the gospel of Jesus Christ breaks down the barriers of skin color and ethnicity. She and I celebrated diversity in our dorm rooms.

One practical way to begin building diversity in your church is to build it within your family through teaching and learning about different cultures and ethnicities throughout the year. Learning the *history* of other cultures can assist you in understanding the *perspective* of other cultures. As you learn with your children, don't limit your knowledge to textbooks and minibiographies. Get creative and cook a new meal. Or introduce your family to the culture and music of those who are different from you.

Invite other Christians into your home for lunches, dinners, or parties. Include members of your church or your neighbors. Find those who are different from you, take an interest in their lives, and invite them over for a meal.

Truthfully, it's more comfortable to dine with those who are just like us, and there is nothing new about that. When the early church gathered in homes—probably the homes of the wealthy—certain divisions emerged over the dinner table (see 1 Corinthians 11:17–22). Commentators believe these divisions were caused because wealthy believers tended to sit and feast together in privileged dining rooms (*triclinium*), while the poorer believers sat in second-class facilities (*atrium*). The privileged Corinthians preferred to dine with those of the same social rank.

But Paul wouldn't stand for it. He challenged the Corinthians regarding these factions, saying, "In the following instructions I do not commend you, because when you come together it is not for the better but for the worse" (1 Corinthians 11:17). Paul doesn't mince words. He would rather they not gather at all than that they gather divided into factions by snobbery. Paul didn't stop there. He went on to say that their elitism was misrepresenting Christ and that their "Lord's supper" was false (v. 20). Paul was appalled by their disregard for the poor among them (vv. 21–22).

Does that sound familiar? It's always more comfortable to dine with people who resemble us, but however comfortable this makes us, divisions over race or class are a clear contradiction of the gospel.

Who can you invite into your home? If you happen to notice visitors at your church, greet them. Be inclusive. Then consider your neighborhood and welcome your neighbors in. Learn about them as people and go beyond skin color or ethnicity, and if their culture is an important aspect of their lives, listen and learn.

Building diversity within the homes of the congregation starts from the heart of the leadership. If pastors are excited and passionate about diversity, the congregation will get a vision for it too. Building diversity in the church begins with pastors who are willing to build diversity into their own homes and make it a priority. Just like parishioners, pastors can begin to take simple steps such as learning history, talking about diversity with their families, and inviting others into their homes.

"Nothing binds a pastor's heart to diversity more than having it in his home," says John Piper.[1] One way Pastor Piper has done this is through adoption, but there are many other important expressions of this principle for pastors to consider. Congregations look to pastors for guidance and direction in their lives. Whether subconsciously or intentionally, we learn from those who lead us in the Lord and emulate their lives.

Pastors themselves must be eager for diversity if we are to see changes in our congregations. But, as with all things, we must not be hasty in casting judgment. Though there may be a desire in the heart of a pastor to pursue diversity, there are real challenges and obstacles in the pursuit of it. We will explore those challenges in chapter 8. But even with the challenges we must not grow complacent. We push forward because of the gospel.

The emphasis here is on congregations, but we make up our congregations, so even if our pastors don't pursue diversity, or if our leadership doesn't emphasize it, that doesn't mean we must wait. We've heard the saying, "Be the change you want to see." If a diverse congregation is a change you'd like to see—and I imagine a welcome one by your pastors—then step out in faith and pursue and invite others.

NOT ABOUT DIVERSITY AFTER ALL

There is one thing that I am assuming, which is that you have a desire to build a home and a church that cultivates diversity. I assume you wouldn't pick up a book about unity and diversity if this wasn't the case. May I submit to you that our pursuit of diversity isn't really about diversity, after all? It's about love. To celebrate diversity in your home, you must first cultivate a love for people—a radical, wholehearted, grace-motivated love for others.

Jesus commands a radical, self-abandoned love, doesn't He? He tells us not only to love others but also to love them as we love ourselves (Matthew 22:37–39). And that's a lot! This type of love God commands of us can only come from one source: Him!

Pray that God would give you a radical love for people, which is what I have prayed and continue to pray for myself. His Word says that if we have not love, we gain nothing (1 Corinthians 13:3). Pray that your heart would be stirred to take an interest in others, in people who are different from you, in people who are also made in the image of God.

Stepping out of our comfort zone is, naturally, uncomfortable. It has been uncomfortable for Christians since the early days of the church in Corinth. It is uncomfortable because our hearts are deceitful (Jeremiah 17:9). It is wise for us to examine our hearts for the sin of partiality.

I believe I briefly mentioned partiality in an earlier chapter, but it's worth reviewing in depth. James addresses partiality when he says:

My brothers, show no partiality as you hold the faith in our Lord Jesus Christ, the Lord of glory. For if a man wearing a gold ring and fine clothing comes into your assembly, and a poor man in shabby clothing also comes in, and if you pay attention to the one who wears the fine clothing and say, "You sit here in a good place," while you say to the poor man, "You stand over there," or, "Sit down at my feet," have you not then made distinctions among yourselves and become judges with evil thoughts? Listen, my beloved brothers, has not God chosen those who are poor in the world to be rich in faith and heirs of the kingdom, which he has promised to those who love him? But you have dishonored the poor man. Are not the rich the ones who oppress you, and the ones who drag you into court? Are they not the ones who blaspheme the honorable name by which you were called? If you really fulfill the royal law according to the Scripture, "You shall love your neighbor as yourself," you are doing well. But if you show partiality, you are committing sin and are convicted by the law as transgressors. (James 2:1–9)

Could it be that you are partial to those who are just like you? Could it be partiality that hinders your pursuit of diversity?

God says that "if we confess our sins, he is faithful and just to forgive us our sins and to cleanse us from all unrighteousness" (1 John 1:9). We can run to God and receive for-giveness and grace. By the grace of God, He will reveal to us what needs to be revealed, and He will give us the grace to repent if repentance is needed; then He will pour out His grace to us again through the forgiveness that comes from knowing Christ.

I'm convinced that diversity is possible if you desire it for your home. If God can bring two people like Liz and me together, then He can definitely create ways for you to serve and love others through diversity until the day when every tongue and tribe will, with one voice, sing praises to our God and King (Revelation 5:9–10).

Until then, let us continue to strive against partiality in our fallen hearts and toward building homes that celebrate diversity, reflecting the diversity of God's people, all for God's glory. We will see that it benefits not only us but also the entire body of Christ. Diversity is beautiful and necessary for our good and the good of others. Amy joins me in this call for diversity when she writes:

> We *need* diversity in the church (in race as well as in age, gender, opinions, marital status, and lifestyle)! No church will ever perfectly exemplify this for different reasons, including that we haven't reached heaven yet, but we can and should try to bring as much of heaven to earth as we can! And it's great for church members to grow in understanding those whose situations they are unfamiliar with. Churches should

desire and pray for diversity because it is God's perfect will and ultimately what heaven will be like.

Lillian adds:

We need diversity! And not just for diversity's sake. All of our differences and various practices help us as the body. We are able to come alongside one another, bringing a fresh perspective, offering various giftings in the Lord, providing fruits of the Spirit where one believer may be weak, another may be strong. We need each other! If we were all the same, practicing the same methods of parenting, schooling, and spiritual disciplines, how could the church body grow? How could God's people be challenged and helped?

My girlfriends came to these conclusions because they benefited from diversity. Diversity wasn't on their radar prior to the three of us meeting together regularly. Through fellowship, mutual love and admiration, and humility they began to see the beauty of what God was doing in our relationships beyond putting together three young girls for dinner and fun. God was building in us something beautiful for His glory. He was using our unique gifts, our specific experiences, and yes, even our ethnicities to teach us more about one another and most importantly more about Him.

CHAPTER 7
HIS BRIDE

YOU MAY BE WONDERING, "Trillia, if you were initially unsure about your church because of the lack of diversity, why did you stay?" I have always seen this as a valid question. Why would I remain someplace where I felt different both in culture and in personal identity? Remember, I hadn't yet understood that my full identity was in Christ. I was still early in my faith, learning and growing in even the basics. The answer for me, though, has always been easy: the church with all its flaws and all its graces has always been my safe place.

Jesus gave Himself up for His bride, the church, and though some might argue that there really isn't a need for a church building or a community of believers, because faith is between the individual and the Lord, I believe God calls Christians into community with fellow Christians. God's Word makes clear that we are to be in fellowship with other believers (Hebrews 10:25). So the church is a fundamental element of the Christian faith. I was aware of my need for a church body even as a new Christian.

Frankly, without the church I would have gone my own way. Faith without community is hard, and I had temptations and doubts that I simply would not have been equipped to handle on my own. I imagine I would never have heard anyone tell me, "Preach the gospel to yourself," and I wouldn't have felt the need to confess my sins. I would have been tempted to adopt a worldly view of living for Christ without many boundaries. I do believe that the Lord sustains believers; He promises to finish the good work He has begun (Philippians 1:6). The Spirit was active in my life; I just know myself, and I know that with enough temptation and no accountability or help, I am at risk of falling. It was the sweet friendships with Lillian and Amy that God tangibly used as a means to sustaining grace. The friendships, which developed in the church first and foremost, were God's gracious gift to me. We weren't just friends; we were also accountable to each other.

As I recounted in chapter 4, beginning in 2001 I had the privilege each and every Friday afternoon to meet with these two women for mutual encouragement and prayer. We did this for several years, and we still remain accountable to one another off and on to this day. The reasons we started meeting were simple. We were young Christians wanting encouragement in our walk with God; we wanted to build deeper, more meaningful friendships with a few women; and we were girls and loved any excuse to hang out and eat together!

They were real friendships. The purpose of our meeting was simple, but the benefits were endless and life-changing.

If you've spent time in church, you've probably heard that we have all sinned and fall short of the glory of God (Romans 3:23). When I first became a Christian, I freely confessed my sin because I was acutely aware of God's grace and forgiveness. I knew the depths of my heart and what it meant to be forgiven much. But then came knowledge, which, coupled with strides in godliness, can lead to pride (1 Corinthians 8:1). As I grew, I began to subtly believe I should "know better" than to sin, as if the temptation to anger or envy was beyond me. Accountability was a good (and regular) reminder that it is okay to be needy for God's grace. It reminded me that I am a sinner and that, because of Jesus, God is faithful to forgive (1 John 1:8–10). Accountability allows us to confess patterns of temptation, and in so doing we are restrained from actual transgression.

Consistent accountability has been a means of God's protection in my life. To this day, though I'm further along in my walk than I was a decade ago, I do not believe I'm incapable of grievous sin (1 Corinthians 10:12). I am a new creation, and I have the Spirit's power, but it's no longer a surprise that when I want to do good, evil is close at hand (Romans 7:21). I'm not so sure that if I hadn't been part of a healthy local church that I would have understood this as fully as I do today. The church isn't simply a place for us to go and hear preaching on Sundays. It's a community for our benefit, even with all of our preferences, differences, and yes,

HOW CAN WE FULFILL THE GREAT COMMISSION TO GO AND MAKE DISCIPLES OF ALL NATIONS IF WE ALL SEEK ONLY CHURCHES IN WHICH WE ARE COMFORTABLE?

even sins. Understanding that we are all batting on the same team (all have sinned) means we can freely share with close friends in the church. It means I can be vulnerable. It means I can be part of a community of people, even those different from me, and relate.

The point and motivation behind church attendance and accountability isn't just to be open about sin and hear the hard words of rebuke. Though the wounds of a friend are a sign of faithfulness, accountability is also for building up and encouraging one another toward God's goodness and grace found in the cross of Christ. My friends and I reminded one another who we are in Christ: equal in value and worth, equal in redemption, uniquely and diversely created by God, completely accepted, daughters of the Most High, and forgiven. We are children of God, though different, and there was a unique joy experienced in being part of the same family. We reminded one another that we know Jesus, that He is ours, and we were His, and that we can draw near to Him and His throne of grace.

Each week we had a choice to extend to one another

grace or judgment. We could display the love and grace that God had already extended through the judgment of Jesus on the cross (Romans 14:13). Each of us had an opportunity to be honest, which we might not have accomplished had we not established the habit (Ephesians 4:25). There were times we needed to extend forgiveness. And yes, as you, too, might have experienced, honest friendship sometimes leads to hurting one another. We also learned to bear with one another as we struggled through seasons of ongoing temptation (Romans 12:16; Colossians 3:13). We also bore one another's burdens in prayer (Galatians 6:2).

That is the power and beauty of the church. Ultimately, God can use such relationships as a means by which He draws us to Himself. Self-sufficiency says we don't need anyone, but humility shouts for help from those God has placed in our lives. At other times, we might think that we just don't need others who are unlike us. Sometimes logistical barriers keep us from being able to expose ourselves to one another, but that is quite different from resisting diversity because, in our pride, we think we are okay relating only to those we already know who are like us. God graciously reminds us that apart from Him, we can do nothing. And one great means of that reminder is the brothers and sisters He puts in our lives. Our relationships were nurtured and developed in the church.

DOCTRINE TRUMPS COMFORT

There are churches that I could run to in which everyone looks like me. That *might* be easier. I could find churches that play songs and worship in the way that most suits my desires or has a preacher who addresses the congregation in my preferred style. But if that church doesn't teach sound doctrine, my soul could be at risk. I want to be in a place in which I know I will be fed the solid Word of God. I continue to be hungry for solid food, but even as a young believer I understood that I needed the gospel spoon-fed to me each week. That kept me returning each Sunday morning. I needed to be reminded that my greatest need is the good news, and that the news of Jesus' redeeming love and resurrection is for today—for *me* today.

Now, let me be clear: when I first became a Christian, I might have been able to find a local church in which everyone looked like me, in which each aspect of the worship was exactly how I'd desire, in which other aspects of church life I could fully relate to, *and* in which sound teaching was proclaimed. But is that really what we are after? How can we fulfill the Great Commission to go and make disciples of all nations if we all seek only churches in which we are comfortable? Does God call me to be comfortable and fulfill all my needs? Even though I was a young Christian, I knew that I wasn't called to be comfortable.

Jesus sacrificed comfort and the throne for us. Jesus was born of a virgin. The God-man lowered Himself into the womb of a woman. Jesus never once defended Himself. He slept in the homes of common people. Jesus is God, the ruler of heaven and earth, the Alpha and the Omega. He is all-powerful. He could have easily put an end to all His sufferings, but He didn't. He didn't to the point of death. He sacrificed all comfort on our behalf.

I am in no way comparing my minor inconveniences to the deep sorrows Jesus felt and experienced. I do, however, want to emulate His devotion to and fellowship with His Father. He was devoted to His call because, ultimately, He was devoted to His Father. He set His eyes on Calvary for the church.

I wasn't perfectly comfortable at all times, but my soul was being fed, and my life was being made richer through my predominantly white church. Jesus' example is compelling because it helps me remember my calling—to love my neighbor as myself and to love my God with all my heart. I'm not meant to do this alone or retreat into a comfortable place. God wants me to be with the body.

My church was not perfect. We had our fair share of problems and struggles. Yet when I experienced the tragedy and pain of miscarriages, church members were there encouraging my faith. When my first baby was born, they were there with food and sweet advice. When I started writing more frequently, they were there with Starbucks gift cards. They have served and loved me. And I'd like to think I have done the same for them. The love of Christ compels me. The love of Christ compelled them.

Members of a church body aren't always going to get along. It is probably safe to assume you've experienced this in some form. As we live real life together, it's inevitable that we will experience conflicts and maybe even real fights. As sinners walk in the light together, there *will* be conflict. As I began to plug into the church and the feelings of a honeymoon began to dissipate, I quickly learned that we weren't always going to agree. But though we didn't always agree, the gospel prevailed. I share this only to stress that though God used the church to mold and grow me, it wasn't always easy. I don't want to give the impression that because I had great friendships and solid teaching, I was always content. I didn't always rejoice in the goodness of God over the differences. As a matter of fact, our differences challenged me from time to time to evaluate my priorities. I could have taken an easy way out several times, but I chose to stay. This was not always easy, but it was worth it.

GOD LOVES THE CHURCH

What if we made the decision to run from uncomfortable situations? I imagine desegregation would have never happened. It's tough for this generation to think of segregation, but let's think about it for a moment. Imagine we are walking down the street in the early 1950s. If you aren't black, we'd probably be walking on opposite sides; we definitely wouldn't be walking side by side in the Deep South. We need to use the restroom, and we see the sign designating which one we can use. It's not divided into male and female; rather, it's colored and white. Now let's imagine that the life we once knew, the life that divided us into classes and divided us by racial distinctions, was stripped away, and we were suddenly told that we must relate to those who are different from us.

That is what happened, and many ran. They fought against desegregation because it was too uncomfortable, because of the sin of racism in their hearts, and because it's what they knew. Given the chance, we might do the same. Thankfully, we don't have to fight that certain fight because civil rights activists fought it for us.

I think many of our problems with church result from running from difficult or uncomfortable situations rather than persevering when necessary. We don't enjoy facing our fears or being placed in challenging circumstances. And the thought that we could actually escape brings great comfort. Why attend a church that doesn't meet all of your felt needs?

"Christ loved the church and gave himself up for her" (Ephesians 5:25). I go to church because God loves the church, and I want to love what God loves. God loves the church universal, God loves the church on a local level, and God loves the mega-church and the little church that meets in a school. God loves the church because the church is made up of people. God displays His love for man through His Son. Christ died and bore wrath and separation from His Father because He loved the world and sought to establish His church (Matthew 16:18). This is easy to see, isn't it? It makes sense reading it here, but sometimes it's just hard to live out.

Yes, God loves the church and shows His undoubtable love through His Son, but am I really called to love something that hurts at times? Yes, I am. We are to "be imitators of God" and "walk in love" (Ephesians 5:1–2). God's call to love is radical. He calls us to love those who hate us, those who persecute us, and those who sin against us. And He says to do it all without any expectation of getting love back (Luke 6:32–36).

That's just hard. I know it. But God calls us to that type of sacrificial love because He first loved us. God can give you and me the grace to love His church.

GOD WANTS ME IN CHURCH

I realize that saying that God wants us in church can be controversial. I'm convinced, though, that God does want us to be with a body of believers. I'm not convinced about how that must look, but it seems clear in Scripture that God calls us to be in fellowship with others. He values the body and encourages us to function as one body with many parts (1 Corinthians 12:18–20). Even in the midst of hardship within the church, we can come together to encourage one another (Hebrews 10:24–25).

It's actually during those hard times that I desire most to run. I don't want to deal with another conflict, insecurity, sinful leader, or instance of facing my own sin. I don't want to wait and work through the pain. And, to be clear, there might be times that I don't have to. We aren't necessarily called to endure and persevere through every situation. In a compelling article entitled, "When You Should Flee Your Church," author Trevin Wax highlighted abusive practices within leadership that are grounds for leaving a church immediately.[1] Referencing a book by Jonathan Leeman, he names twelve things that indicate that a church or its leadership might be abusive. A few include but are not limited to: making dogmatic prescriptions in places where Scripture is silent; relying on intelligence, humor, charm, guilt, emotions, or threats rather than on God's Word and prayer (Acts 6:4); playing favorites; recommending courses of action that always, somehow, improve the leader's own situation, even at the expense of others; and preaching, counseling, discipling, and overseeing the church with lips that fail to ground everything in what Christ has done in the gospel and to give glory to God. Clearly there are times when separation is the best option.

But if I'm searching for the church in which I can be real and share my life with others while others share their lives with me—and in addition be a church that will also meet every single one of my desires at all times—I need not bother going. That church isn't out there. There is no utopia church. Yet I believe God has called us to go and to be real and messy and honest and diverse, to go and learn *how to* endure in love, to go even when it can be uncomfortable—because Jesus died for the church, and there was no greater pain than the pain He endured on our behalf on the cross.

WHAT ABOUT THE REST OF US?

Understanding God's creation and how it applies to the gospel should have an effect on how we view and interact with others—all others but especially those in the church. Theoretically we know this. We know that God created each of us with equal value and worth. We know that the gospel, the good news that Jesus came to seek and save the lost, is for everyone who will believe (Luke 19:10). We know that God calls us to community (or, at least, we hopefully know now).

Yet are we living out these truths?

I'm not highlighting our failure to pursue others in the church or our general desire to be with those like us to cause guilt or condemnation. It's simply a matter of the mission. It's good for us to evaluate our mission—our mission is His mission. What does it mean to go and make disciples of all nations, and how does that relate to us individually? What is hindering us from pursuing the development of multiethnic churches? I have some ideas of what the causes could be, including but not limited to geographical restrictions, homogeneous communities, and well-established churches ingrained in a certain membership demographic. I will dive into the specifics in chapter 8, including why I believe, despite all these hindrances, our pursuit of diversity ultimately gives God glory.

But as we've seen before, "if you really fulfill the royal law according to the Scripture, 'You shall love your neighbor as yourself,' you are doing well. But if you show partiality, you are committing sin and are convicted by the law as transgressors" (James 2:8–9).

I would challenge you to honestly ask yourself if you struggle engaging in this pursuit. No one is immune from the temptation to be partial, and perhaps that's what drives us to certain churches. I, for one, have a favorite coffee shop that I go to, and as different people come and go I can easily find myself making conclusions about them based on their dress or demeanor. It's easy to do. It's easy to wait after church and find someone who looks like you to welcome. I can find myself desiring to speak only with my friends rather than stepping out of my comfort zone and being hospitable. It's comfortable. It's what we know.

Here's what's amazing: we are never tempted without a way of escape (1 Corinthians 10:13), and in this situation we can look to Jesus as our prime example. Besides the fact that Jesus loved the poor, orphans, widows, tax collectors, and prostitutes, He died for those who weren't His friends. His impartiality is the absolute most extreme. His death wasn't just for His friends or for those just like Him (of course we know there is no one like Him). Jesus laid down His life for His enemies. Amazing.

We should look to Jesus and love our neighbors as ourselves by laying down our comforts to reach out to those unlike us and to walk in love and maybe even attend the same church. This will not be easy. But it is part of the mission.

Any change is enabled only by God's Spirit and by His grace. We must step out in faith, but God is the one who supplies the grace. We must make the effort, but God is our strength. Perhaps some of the first steps we can take in our pursuit of diversity are as follows:

- **Pray.** No matter the demographic of your church, you can begin to pray that God would give you opportunities to reach out to those unlike yourself. God loves the prayers of His saints. Ask Him to bring diversity across your path. Ask Him to give you wisdom and grace for diverse relationships.

- **Evangelize.** We can't really go and make disciples of all nations without sharing the gospel. Ask God to provide opportunities to boldly proclaim Christ to those around you. Get uncomfortable. Step out in faith to reach those unlike you. As I've mentioned before, diversity isn't about diversity for diversity's sake; it's about the gospel and spreading that news to all people.
- **Hospitality.** In chapter 6 we saw how we might build diversity in our homes. Seek opportunities to apply those suggestions.
- **Go.** We can be a people who will go and choose to go to churches that are attempting to build multiethnic congregations.
- **Stay.** We can stay in situations that may be uncomfortable yet are good, because we believe the Lord has us there for the purpose of building His church, even if we are lonely snowflakes.

The gospel broke the barriers that would have driven me out of my church. God captured my heart with His vision for diversity for the church and planted my feet on solid ground. As a result, I and the other church members benefited during those days of worshiping together. Today, this church is diverse. The Lord has been faithful to fill it with a variety of ethnicities. What a beautiful thing. I'm thankful I endured and waited to watch the Lord answer my prayers. He is faithful and will build His church, our safe place.

CHAPTER 8
A DIFFICULT PURSUIT

GOD LOVES DIVERSITY. Diversity has been on display from the moment He began creating the world. I love the creation account. In the beginning God created day and night. He made stars, each with its unique makeup. He created animals that crawl and jump and fly. He created papayas and watermelon and trees that blossom into apples. And we know He created man. He is a creative God. And God shows His ultimate love for diversity in the cross of Christ; Christ died for *every* tongue and tribe, and on the last day *every* tribe and tongue will be represented worshiping Him. To be able to reflect that day *today* would show the heart of God as seen throughout Scripture and reveal His glory to the world. As we have seen, though it was only a small glimpse, the diversity of my friendships with Lillian and Amy have mirrored that day for His glory.

My hope is that in reading *United*, your eyes have been opened to what I believe is the heart of God for diversity.

What I am after as I share the beauty of diversity in the church is one thing and one thing only: the glory of God. I don't want the church to find yet another trendy pursuit to latch on to. The pursuit of diversity is important, yes, but not because it's trendy, this generation's "hip thing." It's important because the nations fill God's world. Seeing the importance of diversity in Scripture should make us want to explore how we can emulate this today. Ultimately it's all about His glory on this earth and reflecting Him to a broken world.

But there are difficult realities and facts that we must face in this pursuit; change is difficult, and the prospect of building diversity in the church may come with great challenges. There are also other compelling reasons why we can't afford to ignore the need or even the potential for a forced integration. Because our nation is changing, churches may be forced to integrate without much effort or pursuit. Theological convictions or tradition will cause many to search out churches that might be predominantly white. Integration that is forced by conviction is passive, and although it lacks intentionality, it could happen. For this reason and others, we need to be aware of the changing demographics in our nation.

The world is ever changing, and although the United States continues to become less homogeneous, our churches have not. In March 2012, the *Wall Street Journal* reported that minorities now account for more than half the babies born in America, noting that it's "a milestone in the path toward what demographers forecast will be an overall majority-minority population in 30 years."[1] In June 2013, the *Washington Post* published that more white people died in the United States in 2012 than were born, noting in a previous article that this finding is "a surprising slump coming more than a decade before the Census Bureau says that the ranks of white Americans will likely drop with every passing year."[2] Yet despite all of these cultural changes, our churches remain mostly segregated, separated into ethnic groups.

In June of 2012, Ed Stetzer, president of Lifeway Research, reported his findings on changes in the ethnic and racial landscape of the American church. Stetzer found that there are certain denominations making significant gains within their ranks in terms of greater diversity. Stetzer's report does not suggest that these congregations are increasingly multiethnic; rather, the percentage of all-white congregations within certain denominations is decreasing.[3] As the landscape of the United States changes, I imagine we will see more ethnically diverse churches. And if the leadership of many of these churches remains white, these leaders need to take note of such changes.

Having read the previous chapters of this book, it will come as no surprise to you that this is important to me, but I want to reiterate why I hope you'll also be captured by what I believe is God's vision for diversity. Again, for me it goes back to God's Word. I find that the picture given for churches seems to be one made up of multiethnic, multicultural, and economically varying individuals.

In Mark 11:17 we see Jesus quoting Isaiah as He teaches in the temple, asking: "Is it not written, 'My house shall be called a house of prayer for all the nations'?" (see also Isaiah 56:7). Jesus is cleaning house, so to speak, ridding the temple of corruption so that it would be a place for *all* nations. Paul adds a word about socioeconomic elitism in 1 Corinthians when he rebukes the Corinthians for superiority at the Lord's Supper. Paul urges them not to humiliate those who have nothing (11:22). And Christians are charged to go and make disciples of *all* nations (Matthew 28:16–20). Finally, we know that at the end of time, as we all look on the face of Jesus, we will be surrounded by a multitude of nations made up of all tongues, tribes, and peoples (Revelation 7:9).

It's a beautiful picture of what God intended for the church. Please don't misunderstand here. I am not saying that churches that are not diverse are lesser than multiethnic churches or disobedient to God's Word. But with that said, I do believe we can ask the question: Why aren't they experiencing or encouraging diversity? Though I don't pretend to be able to point to one clear, concrete fact and name it as the only possibility, I do have some ideas about why this might be the case. I'd even go so far as to say it is much less complicated than we might think.

I want to briefly share a few thoughts on factors that may hinder a pursuit of diversity.

A DIFFICULT ROAD

Geographical restrictions can hinder our pursuit of diversity. If you plan to plant a church in rural Appalachia, for example, where, according to the Appalachian Regional

Commission, the population is 83.9 percent white, you may have a difficult time reaching "all nations."[4] Rural towns need the gospel just as much as diverse cities, so we shouldn't restrict our pursuit to apply the Great Commission to those who live in a particular area. It's merely a fact that we must know and understand—some locations in and of themselves are not diverse to begin with. So it makes sense that the churches found in these areas won't be either.

With that said, we can't ignore the fact that cities are growing. In a 2013 interview Matt Smethurst conducted with Stephen Um, coauthor of *Why Cities Matter*, he opened with some remarkable statistics about city growth. Smethurst wrote, "Like it or not, it's true: more people are living in cities than ever before. This migration cityward doesn't appear to be waning, either; in fact, it's projected that within the next 35 years our world will be 70 percent urban. (In 1800, that number was 2 percent. In 1900, it was 14 percent.)"[5]

Trying to stress the importance of cities, Um and his coauthor, Justin Buzzard, wrote that "cities are diverse, dense places where different types of people interact with one another. Cities are populated with people of various cultures, different worldviews, and different vocations. Cities force individuals to refine their cultural assumptions, religious beliefs, and sense of calling as they run up against the sharp edges of the assumptions, beliefs, and expertise of other city dwellers."[6]

The comparison of cities to the rural area is in no way to pit the two against each other. I cannot stress this enough—God doesn't command that our mission be isolated to one area or one kind of place. Such thinking is anti–gospel mission. But we can't ignore population growth, just as we can't ignore the demographical changes in our country.

Though cities are experiencing tremendous growth, there remain homogeneous communities within them that make it difficult to pursue diversity. It's not just in rural locations that we find like communities living together. The reality is, these communities build churches, and therefore we have homogeneous churches in homogeneous neighborhoods even inside of diverse cities. This lack of context could be contributed to our segregated neighborhoods and churches. A 2012 article in *U.S. News Weekly* reported on a study conducted by researchers at Dartmouth, the University of Georgia, and the University of Washington, which revealed that not much had changed from the segregated times brought on by the Jim Crow laws. Unsurprisingly, the study found that African-Americans remain concentrated in segregated neighborhoods and that diverse neighborhoods are rare. It also discovered that immigrants tend to populate among themselves as well. The result is concentrated pockets of ethnic groups. Here is an excerpt of the article explaining the study's findings, using the city of Atlanta as a guide:

> In 1990, the city was predominantly white and black. Of a total of 658 tracts (neighborhoods) in 1990, 398 neighborhoods were classified as low-diversity, white-dominant, while 112 were low-diversity, black-dominant tracts. "Atlanta was archetypically white

suburbs and an African-American central city, something you would see in Detroit, Pittsburgh, or Cincinnati today," Wright said.

Over the next 20 years in Atlanta, the generally all-white neighborhoods shrank dramatically, according to the research by Wright, Steven Holloway at the University of Georgia, and Mark Ellis from the University of Washington. The 116 remaining low-diversity, white-dominant neighborhoods in Atlanta in 2010 now represent just 17 percent of all neighborhoods in Atlanta, compared to 60 percent 20 years ago.

However, the number of low-diversity, black-dominant neighborhoods in Atlanta actually increased from 112 in 1990 to 123 in 2000. And while the number decreased slightly to 115 in 2010, that still means that, over the past two decades, the number of generally all-black neighborhoods increased overall in Atlanta over the past 20 years.[7]

Such statistics reveal how seldom people interact (as far as home life) with those outside their specific ethnic group. People of the same background and ethnicity tend to relate to and be most comfortable with each other. That makes sense. I remember as a young child finding the one black girlfriend I knew in my school to see if I could eat with her during lunch. But is this mentality best for the church?

Some would argue, and understandably so, that it wouldn't

benefit a Korean-speaking community to come to a church in which they couldn't understand the English sermon. I agree. I see the need for and importance of multi-language ministries or churches to serve the needs of foreign communities. But we must be careful not to use our differences in language and culture as a crutch or an excuse. We also must not allow our differences to be excuses for apathy. It's simply easier to coast through life not worrying about anyone outside of those immediately associated with us. It takes effort to know those not like us, to study history and ask hard questions and be willing to change. I do not discount the potential need for a Korean community (for example) to build a church that specifically meets their needs, but I would venture to say that more often than not, we choose apathy before we aggressively seek to learn about others.

Along with communities that are historically segregated, there are also long-standing churches that may have a difficult time pursuing diversity. Churches that have been established for hundreds of years (or perhaps even as few as fifty) may have a difficult time changing a church culture that has been in existence for so long. Must they change? If it's a long-standing, well-established church, surely they're okay the way they are. I would argue, however, that a pursuit to diversify is always a worthwhile endeavor. It sends a message to the world, which includes your neighbor, that you are willing to love others as you love yourself (Luke 10:27). Pursuing those different from us allows us the chance to go to war against the sin of partiality (James 2:9). And, again, this pursuit gives us the opportunity to live out the Great Commission. But it isn't necessary for every thriving ministry. Sometimes long-standing, homogeneous churches may do better sending others out to plant or support churches that are more equipped for multiethnic ministry.

If there is a long-standing church that's filled with sixty- to eighty-year-olds who may not be equipped to reach our generation but who have resources to support and send others, I think those members should make an effort to do so. It is not an inferior ministry opportunity but a chance to carry out the Great Commission. Such churches struggle to change, from a demographical standpoint. It's not impossible; however, a church that has limited service opportunities but a heart for diversity should train up and send.

In contrast, let's say there is a midsized, predominantly white church that's been around for a while and is involved in some good ministry to youth and families. Its members have heard that diversity is important and have been convicted of a lack of outreach to those unlike themselves, but instead of doing something about it internally, they find a black church nearby and maybe visit once a year and consider diversity checked off the list. They *could* change and pursue diversity, but they figure they'll just throw in some time and maybe support them financially to some degree (if it's needed), and that covers the bases.

In order for any substantial change to occur and be sustained, it starts with church leadership. The leadership doesn't necessarily need to implement the change, although

I do believe that is extremely important. What I have in mind is the makeup of leadership teams within our churches. The leadership of many of our evangelical churches and denominations remains white. Schools such as the Reformed Theological Seminary in Jackson, Mississippi, are working hard to recruit African-Americans in order to equip them for leadership primarily within the Presbyterian Church in America, but there remains a gap. Why do you think it was such big news that, in 2012, the Southern Baptist Convention elected an African-American president, Fred Luter Jr.? News sources from every end of the spectrum ran the story, including the *New York Times*.[8] Why? Because almost four decades after the civil rights movement, the largest Protestant denomination finally elected a black leader. This was truly breathtaking and encouraging news. We have come so far, but clearly we have not arrived. There's still work to be done. I believe that if we're not captivated by God's vision for diversity, the chances are strong that we will not see a significant difference in the ethnicity of our leadership in our lifetime.

Is pursuing diversity difficult? The answer is yes, very. So, what's the point? If it's difficult, and if neighborhood demographics are such that at times it is made almost impossible, why do we do it? You've likely heard the saying, "Anything worth having is worth fighting for." Diversity is worth having because diversity is about people, and people are worth fighting for. If God is mindful of man, shouldn't we be (Psalm 8:3–4)?

Reflect on that. God, who created the heavens, is mindful of us. God, who delighted in His Son, sent His Son to die for us. As a result, we, too, should be mindful of men. I think that's why God gives us two commandments related to our interaction with other people: love your neighbor as yourself, and go and make disciples of all nations. He thinks of us. He loves us. We are even created in His very image. The gospel motivates us to pursue diversity despite all the obstacles.

CHAPTER 9

FOR OUR KIDS

MARTIN LUTHER KING'S "I Have a Dream" speech is probably the most referenced speech when addressing issues of race and ethnicity, and it is one of the most popular speeches of all time. His vision and hope for the future, at the time, seemed an impossible feat. He captured the audience and the hearts of many as he envisioned little black boys and girls joining hands with little white boys and girls as sisters and brothers.

It was the summer of 1963, and unlike the vast majority of days, this one would go down in history as the day that two hundred thousand people rallied together in Washington to listen to leaders address the issues facing blacks at that time.[1] The event was solidified in the history books as Martin Luther King began his famous speech:

Five score years ago, a great American, in whose symbolic shadow we stand today, signed the Emancipation Proclamation. This momentous decree came as a great beacon light of hope to millions of Negro slaves who had been seared in the flames of withering injustice. It came as a joyous daybreak to end the long night of their captivity.

But it's these words of his in particular that resonated with the nation, and it's these words that penetrate my heart now:

I have a dream that one day, down in Alabama, with its vicious racists, with its governor having his lips dripping with the words of "interposition" and "nullification"—one day right there in Alabama little black boys and black girls will be able to join hands with little white boys and white girls as sisters and brothers.[2]

Yes, as sisters and brothers. Dr. King's dream was of sisters and brothers united in humanity, yet, as I described earlier, we know that we who are in Christ are already sisters and brothers. The dream and vision of human equality has become a slight reality. Slight, insofar as some might argue that various systems such as welfare have hindered the advancement of minority groups. Nevertheless, our government no longer restricts any race access to public spaces by its laws. We are free in America to go about as we wish. We can walk hand in hand with little or no fear of retaliation. We can eat and drink together in the same facility, and we are free to marry one another. That's pretty radical compared to 1963, only fifty years earlier, when Dr. King first spoke those words.

I'm thankful for his vision and his fight. It's because of it that my husband and I can now walk down the street holding hands and swing our beautiful biracial children without much fear. Interracial marriage is on the rise. A Pew Research Center poll released in February 2012 found that in 2010, 15 percent of all new marriages in the United States were between spouses of different races or ethnicities.[3] That's compared to 6.7 percent in 1980.

In general, interracial marriage is no longer taboo—although some still find it objectionable. While 43 percent of Americans believe it is good for society, there's still 11 percent who believe the growth in interracial marriage is a change for the worse. In December of 2011, a church in Kentucky barred an interracial couple from worshiping together (that ban was eventually overturned due to widespread outrage).[4] And with a quick search on the Web, I discovered many sites and articles arguing the viewpoint that interracial marriage is actually unbiblical. Although this viewpoint exists, pastors have spoken out against it. The evangelical pastor John Piper not only advocates for interracial marriage in his book *Bloodlines*, but he has also has taken the time to preach about the topic.[5]

There's always room for kingdom work as it relates to embracing different ethnicities. I am, however, thankful for the increased acceptance of interracial marriages. That is my marriage. Each morning, my husband and I greet each other with a kiss. His rosy cheeks and fair skin come close to my milk-chocolate tone (as my son likes to say) and curly hair. My husband is white, and I am black. We don't wake up and notice the difference of our skin color; frankly, we go most of our days without a thought about it. But every so often, someone else will remind us—like the time when we were dating, and we stepped out of a restaurant hand in hand. The black couple standing next to the car adjacent to ours wasn't amused by our public display of affection. Not only was "sellout" the message in their looks, but also it came off the male's lips toward me. And then there was the time we visited Memphis, Tennessee, and ate at a nice restaurant in a suburban area. I was most definitely the oddball, and the glares helped remind Thern and me that we weren't welcome.

Because racism still exists, there are times my husband needs to play a protective role in our marriage. There are certain places we may choose not to go. When we've been heckled or glared at in the past, I know my husband supports me as he grips my hand and draws me in closer to himself. His act of protecting and guarding is a display of sacrificial love. When others acknowledge our difference in skin color, he stands ready to die in my stead.

Interracial marriage may be growing in acceptance now among the general population, but it has always been acceptable to God. As we saw earlier, in Numbers 12:1–10, God severely punished Miriam and Aaron for criticizing Moses's marrying a Cushite (Ethiopian) woman. Interracial marriage isn't merely acceptable; it reflects the beauty and glory of the gospel.

When I think of the gospel, I think of reconciliation, peace, unity, acceptance, redemption, and forgiveness. At salvation we are reconciled to God and have peace by the blood of Christ. We are united now with Christ and accepted by God fully through His grace. We are redeemed and have complete forgiveness of sins. It is amazing grace! There's an earthly union that has similar descriptions as the gospel. It falls short of redemption but displays the power of the gospel and the glory of God in the lives of Christians. When

WILL MY KIDS BE ABLE TO SAY WITHOUT A DOUBT—WITH FULL ASSURANCE—THAT THEY ARE LOVED AND CHERISHED BY THE CHURCH BECAUSE THE CHURCH KNOWS THAT THE DIVIDING LINES OF HOSTILITY HAVE BEEN BROKEN BY THE GOSPEL OF JESUS CHRIST?

two people from different ethnicities take the sacred step to become one flesh in marriage, God's gospel is on display.

Like my friendships with Lillian and Amy, my marriage is yet another sweet display of God's beautiful diversity. And from my marriage I have the privilege of raising and loving two biracial babies. Their lives motivate me to think about the future.

OUR CHILDREN

Dr. King's vision for diversity doesn't compare to the grandeur of God's vision for diversity. While Dr. King's speech remains one of the most important historical events in US history (and rightfully so), we see in Scripture that God's view infiltrates all of life and has eternal value. God's view for diversity touches salvation, marriage, and relationships, all affected by God's great grace for the nations. So, like Dr. King in his famous speech, when I think about this pursuit of diversity, I can't help but think primarily of what my children will experience.

In looking at the world around us, I think it's fair to say that society is embracing a life of integration, even if we're not completely there yet. I'm not concerned about whether my children will be accepted by others in the world, mostly because I pray that their security would be in Christ and not in the opinions of man. But another reason I'm not concerned is that American society is tolerant of race in general. We've fought for diversity in our society and have won in many ways. Some might disagree with that for various reasons, yet we can't deny just how far we've come. We no longer must use separate restrooms, for starters. But I want to go back to where we started: what about the church?

Will my kids be able to say without a doubt—with full

assurance—that they are loved and cherished by the church because the church knows that the dividing lines of hostility have been broken by the gospel of Jesus Christ? Will my children feel the love of Christ as they step foot in churches in our nation? Will my kids be able to celebrate that they are uniquely made as white and black and celebrate those differences while also embracing their sameness in creation and redemption?

Dr. King's vision for society should be our vision for ministry in the church—little white and black boys and girls worshiping together, loving each other, attending church together. (Our nation was divided racially primarily between blacks and whites, but we know that God's Word addresses all nations, all ethnicities, and that is the togetherness I'm aiming for.) I'm not alone in asserting a need for diversity. It seems that this topic has gotten new life in recent years, which brings me hope for the future. Books such as *Reconciliation Blues* by Edward Gilbreath, *Aliens in the Promised Land*, edited by Anthony Bradley, and *Bloodlines* by John Piper all address diversity in various ways.[6] It's an important topic, and one that won't go away until Jesus returns.

The unfortunate effect of the fall is that sin will remain until all things are made new. This means that racial division and struggles will remain until that day. But it doesn't mean that by God's grace and through His power, the effects of the fall can't be pushed back. In other words, Christ breaks the power of canceled sin.[7] We don't have to succumb to sin. It's no longer our master. So there really and truly is hope for us and our kids! They can know a church that, while not sinless, is fighting against the temptation to be divided and partial. The church can't be complacent in order to make these changes; it must be on the offensive, active and intentional.

My dream and hope is that my black-and-white children (the sweet gift of biracial blood) will be holding hands with black, Latino, Chinese, European, and African children in church one day, worshiping together. Stop and think about that. Isn't it a beautiful picture? My dream is that they would not have to wonder if the church they attend will reject them because of the color of their skin. My dream is that as they enter into adulthood, they will wonder why their mother thought a book about diversity, friendship, and the church was needed. I hope it will seem a silly notion, and that when they are parents, it will seem as impossible to imagine as it is difficult for me to imagine segregation today.

Though many years have passed since the day Dr. King spoke about his famous dream, racial reconciliation remains a present need. My prayer is that as we pursue diversity through building relationships with those who are unlike us in the church, we will be able to retire that saying we know so well: "Sunday mornings are the most segregated hour of the week." I want us to make that a thing of the past. May it be that the dream would fade into reality, that the dream of the beautifully diverse church would be the reality for my kids. Let's pave the way so that one day our children will be worshiping together, celebrating their differences and unity as God's family in a powerful and beautiful way.

APPENDIX

INTERVIEW ON THE TOPIC OF RACE WITH THABITI ANYABWILE

THABITI ANYABWILE IS THE senior pastor of First Baptist Church of Grand Cayman and the author of or contributor to seventeen books. Pastor Anyabwile would like to rid the world of the notion of race. Here is a recent Q&A I did with him where he explains his reasoning.

When and how did you begin to determine that race is nonexistent?

ANYABWILE: I'm pretty much like everyone else I know. I assumed that "racial" categories in some way were rooted in our biology or genetics. It seemed obvious to me. I am black, others are white, and so on. Growing up, we didn't question "race" as a category. Instead, we fought very hard to make "blackness" meaningful and dignified. It was a matter of pride and resistance against the negative images and tropes in the wider culture. So the project was to define *blackness* in a way that gave it a historically and socially positive meaning that would motivate more striving for excellence.

I began my academic study of race as a graduate student in psychology. My master's research focused on the development of racial identity attitudes—what attitudes and feelings people associated with their race and how those feelings developed through four or five phases. That's when I began to see that race really is a social and psychological construction. And that's when I began to suspect that once we enter the labyrinth of race, there is no way to exit. Race has become this quicksand of our own making. If we accept the construct and struggle against it, then we will simply find ourselves immersed more deeply. It was an intuitive realization, and it stuck.

Is it accurate to say that you believe the term *race* is man-made or invented? Where do you believe the term *race* comes from?

ANYABWILE: Yes. *Race* works its way into our common thought and language following the work of four men: French physician Francois Bernier (1620–1688), Swedish professor of botany Carolus Linnaeus (1707–1778), French natural historian George Louis Leclerc Buffon (1707–1778), and German professor of medicine Johann Friedrich Blumenbach (1752–1840). In 1684 Bernier published the first work categorizing humanity into four groups: Europeans, Far Easterners, blacks, and Lapps. In 1735 Linnaeus published a work that was the first to use color in classifying humanity. He had four groups as well: Europeans (white), Asians (yellow), Africans (black), and Americans (red). Buffon was the first to formally classify people into races, in 1778. He imagined six races:

Europeans, Lapps, Tartars, South Asians, Ethiopians, and Americans. Finally, Blumenbach published a work that went through a couple of editions. It probably had the longest-lasting effect when it comes to introducing race into our worldview. He put people into five races based on a physical-anthropological scheme: Caucasian, Mongolian, Ethiopian, American, and Malaysian.

We get the word *Caucasian* from Blumenbach, who found a skull in the Caucasus area of Russia and argued that the region "produces the most beautiful race of men, I mean the Georgian." He wrongly concluded that the region was the cradle of humanity. By this time it's painfully evident that certain attitudes are being attached to physical characteristics. That constellation of some physical characteristics and associated attitudes is what we commonly refer to as "race." The idea doesn't really enter and dominate human worldviews until the seventeenth and eighteenth centuries, which, not coincidentally, was also the period of colonial expansion, slavery's expansion, and increased contact between peoples. Race, which starts as a pseudoscientific classification, eventually gets deployed as a theory to explain human difference and human supremacy, an explanation needed to justify the conquering of people groups around the world.

If race is nonexistent or an error, what would you say are the proper terms for describing who we are as God's created creatures?

ANYABWILE: On the one hand, it doesn't matter which term we choose if we don't deconstruct the underlying ideas that give us *race*. It turns out that racial thinking is rather stubborn. We could put random letters together as a substitute—say, "arnvnwohf"—and we'd fill that nonsense word with all the assumptions of race. That's what we do with the term *ethnicity*. Most people think you're talking about race under a synonym. That's a mistake. What we're *not* suggesting is that we simply need better words.

What we *are* suggesting is that we need to deconstruct the assumptions and ideology of race in order to reconstruct a biblical identity. That's a lot of work and not easily explained in this short interview. But imagine tearing an old barn down board by board, tossing the boards eaten by termites and too weather-beaten to be used, before rebuilding the barn with the best of what's left and some fresh lumber from the mill. That's what we need to do with our identity. The word the Bible uses is *ethne*, meaning "nations" or "people group" or "ethnicity." But that's a use of "ethnicity" that's flat-out contrary to "race." The key proof texts would be Genesis 10 and Acts 17:26. Both those texts teach our common ancestry in Adam and Eve. They teach our close cousinage, as Colin Kidd puts it in *The Forging of Races*, not our differing species as race theory originally argued.

So, I'd opt for a biblical term with a biblical definition. That term is *ethnicity*, properly understood.

In a recent exchange, you explained that ethnicity or being defined by different ethnicities is more accurate than race. Would you elaborate?

ANYABWILE: When we read the Bible, one useful question

to ask ourselves is: What story is the Bible telling me about the origin of humanity and its diversity? When we ask that question, we see several things. First, Eve is "the mother of all the living" (Genesis 3:20 NIV). Second, several generations later, the human line is narrowed again to one family, that of Noah and his sons (Genesis 6–9). All the families of the earth are descended from Noah's three sons and their wives (Genesis 10). "From these the nations spread out over the earth after the flood" (v. 32 NIV). These "nations" are not national city-states, but "clans and languages, in their territories." In other words, these are large kinship and language groups. The story the Bible tells is one of *continuity*, not discontinuity, which "race" at least implies. So you get the pronouncement of Acts 17:26—"From one man he made every nation of men, that they should inhabit the whole earth" (NIV).

This is the way the Bible speaks of our common ancestry and of the ethnic diversity we seek. It's a diversity within the same species, if you will. In fact, genetic science has proven that there are no subspecies in mankind. There's not enough genetic variance to meet the tests of science.

So it's most proper to speak of *ethnicities* rather than of *races*. That matters for several reasons. First, it allows us to emphasize our common humanity and kinship. Second, ethnicities are malleable and permeable. They arise out of other groups (take Israel arising from one pagan man), and they can be entered into by people who were not originally a part of the group (through marriage, for example). So we have a category that's not bounded by biology or race, and that makes more sense of our experience. Think of the famous census question on race. We should all check "other." Third, ethnicity—with its constellation of kinship, language, and culture—allows us to discuss critical differences in culture and worldview without implicating one another as racists.

If my culture is a product of my race, then by definition anyone who questions my culture implicates himself as a racist. Also, if we don't detangle *culture* from *race* as biology, then any discussion of the merits of one culture versus another leads us into the notions of supremacy based on race. This is why so many of our discussions of race and culture break down into accusations of racism and uneasy feelings of superiority and inferiority. We find ourselves being accused of things we don't necessarily think or believe, and yet we can't find another way to say what we think or believe that doesn't lead to conflict. That's because *race* implicates us all. But ethnicity properly understood frees us from wrong biological assumptions and allows us to discuss difference in a less explosive way.

You are on a quest to rid the culture of the term *race*. What do you think would happen if you accomplished this goal?

ANYABWILE: Well, not just the term. We need to rid ourselves of the underlying assumptions, preferences, and ideologies. We're hurting ourselves and each other by leaving those things unexamined. My hope would be to see a world that really is "post-racial" because it really has understood, deconstructed, and subsequently reconstructed human identity along biblical lines. I'm fighting for our sanity. We can't live contrary to God's design and definition of us without, in fact, losing our minds and our souls. "Racializing" our worlds is one way we lose ourselves. That's why it's profoundly important that we understand the renewal Jesus has achieved for us. That renewal includes the ability to see ourselves as a renewed humanity, not only with common ancestry in Adam but now with a common union in Jesus Christ. He has freed us from the laws of race and racism, just as He has freed us from the law of sin and death. I want everyone to discover the joy and healing of that freedom. If we could accept it, I think we'll see deeper levels of peace, understanding, cooperation, sharing, and partnership across ethnic groups in Christ. In other words, we'd really be the church, and the church would include an increasing share of the world. That's my hope.

THABITI ANYABWILE'S RECOMMENDED READING

Graves, Joseph L. *The Race Myth: Why We Pretend Race Exists in America*. New York: Plume, 2005.

Hayes, Daniel J. *From Every Tribe and Nation: A Biblical Theology of Race*. Downers Grove, IL: InterVarsity, 2003.

Kidd, Colin. *The Forging of Races: Race and Scripture in the Protestant Atlantic World, 1600–2000*. New York: Cambridge University Press, 2006.

Sharp, Douglas R. *No Partiality: The Idolatry of Race and the New Humanity*. Downers Grove, IL: InterVarsity, 2002.

Ulander, Dave. *Shattering the Myth of Race: Genetic Realities and Biblical Truths*. Valley Forge, PA: Judson Press, 2000.

Williams, Jarvis J. *One New Man: The Cross and Racial Reconciliation in Pauline Theology.* Nashville: B&H Academic, 2010.

NOTES

Introduction

1. John Piper, *Bloodlines: Race, Cross, and the Christian* (Wheaton, IL: Crossway, 2011), Kindle edition, conclusion.
2. Ibid.

Chapter 1: My New Identity

1. "Rodney King," The Biography Channel, www.biography.com/people/rodney-king-9542141 (accessed July 27, 2013).
2. Hanna Bordas, "Desegregation Now. Segregation Tomorrow?" Harvard Graduate School of Education (2006), www.gse.harvard.edu/news_events/ed/2006/summer/features/resegregation.html.
3. John Piper, "Class, Culture and Ethnic Identity in Christ," *Desiring God* (blog), January 17, 1999, www.desiringgod.org/resource-library/sermons/class-culture-and-ethnic-identity-in-christ.
4. Elyse M. Fitzpatrick, *Because He Loves Me: How Christ Transforms Our Daily Life* (Wheaton, IL: Crossway, 2008), 54.

Chapter 2: *My* White Church

1. In recent years, as my church has sought to reach out beyond its immediate community, we've seen an influx in the number of minorities who attend. Glory to God!
2. An idol is anything you desire or worship more than God. Idolatry can rule your thoughts and actions.

Chapter 3: Longing for Diversity

1. Christian McWhirter, "The Birth of 'Dixie," *New York Times*, March 31, 2013, http://opinionator.blogs.nytimes.com/2012/03/31/the-birth-of-dixie/.

2. "Slavery in America," History.com, www.history.com/topics/slavery (accessed July 27, 2013).

3. Lynne Olson, *Freedom's Daughters: The Unsung Heroines of the Civil Rights Movement from 1830 to 1970* (New York: Scribner, 2002), 35.

4. Monergism.com has published a thorough sampling of articles that address Reformed theology (www.monergism.com/thethreshold/ sdg/classic.html). For additional information and definition, consult the Westminster Confession, which has been provided online by Westminster Theological Seminary (www.wts.edu/resources/creeds/ westminsterconfession.html). Other organizations that prove helpful in exploring Reformed theology include but are not limited to Ligonier Ministries, The Gospel Coalition, and Desiring God.

5. John Piper, *Bloodlines: Race, Cross, and the Christian* (Wheaton, IL: Crossway, 2011), Kindle edition, appendix 3.

6. Anthony Carter, *On Being Black and Reformed: A New Perspective on the African American Christian Experience* (Phillipsburg, NJ: P&R, 2003), Kindle edition, chap. 1.

7. Some ideas include a fish fry, card party, and yes, a brunch—just not *only* brunches.

8. Piper, *Bloodlines*, chap. 11.

Chapter 4: God's Provision of Diversity

1. C. S. Lewis, *The Weight of Glory* (New York: HarperOne, 2009), 45.

2. J. Daniel Hays, *From Every People and Nation: A Biblical Theology of Race* (Downers Grove, IL: InterVarsity, 2003), 48. J. Daniel Hays references three books (pp. 52–54) still in print and available at popular sites such as Amazon and Christian Book Distributors (CBD): Arthur W. Pink, *Gleaning in Genesis* (1922; repr. Chicago: Moody, 1950); C. F. Keil and Franz Delitzsch, *Commentary on the Old Testament* (Grand Rapids, MI: Eerdmans, 1986); *The Preacher's Homiletic Commentary*, 31 vols. (1892; repr. Grand Rapids, MI: Baker, 1980).

3. Hays, *From Every People and Nation,* 48–49.

4. Ibid., 53.

5. Ibid., 55.

6. Thabiti Anyabwile, "Where Does Blackness and Whiteness Come From?" January, 26, 2012, http://thegospelcoalition.org/blog /thabitianyabwile/2012/01/26/where-does-blackness-and-whiteness-come-from/.

Chapter 5: Different but the Same

1. Geneva Smitherman, *Black Talk* (Boston: Houghton Mifflin, 1994), 207.
2. John Piper, "Foundations for Thinking about Race," Desiring God, January 16, 1996, www.desiringgod.org/resource-library/taste-see-articles/foundations-for-thinking-about-race.
3. Ibid.
4. Russell Moore, *Adopted for Life* (Wheaton: IL, Crossway, 2009), Kindle edition, chap. 2.

Chapter 6: Growing Together in Christ

1. John Piper, *Bloodlines: Race, Cross, and the Christian* (Wheaton, IL: Crossway, 2011), Kindle edition, chap. 1.

Chapter 7: His Bride

1. Trevin Wax, "When You Should Flee Your Church," April 24, 2012, http://thegospelcoalition.org/blogs/trevinwax/2012/04/24/when-you-should-not-submit/.

Chapter 8: A Difficult Pursuit

1. "America's Changing Demographics," *Washington Post*, May 17, 2012, http://articles.washingtonpost.com/2012-05-17/opinions/35458398_1_unauthorized-immigrants-illegal-immigrants-immi-grant-pool.
2. Carol Morello and Ted Mellnik, "White Deaths Outnumber Births for First Time," *Washington Post*, June 12, 2013, www.washingtonpost.com/local/white-deaths-outnumber-births-for-first-time/2013/06/13/3bb1017c-d388-11e2-a73e-826d299ff459_story.html.
3. Ed Stetzer, "Changing Ethnic and Racial Landscape," *Christianity Today*, June 2012, www.christianitytoday.com/edstetzer/2012/june/changing-ethinic-and-racial-landscape-of-denomoninations.html.
4. "Race and Hispanic Origin" Appalachian Regional Commission, Report 2007–2011, www.arc.gov/assets/research_reports/PRBDataOverviewReport2007-2011-Chapter3.pdf.
5. Matt Smethurst, "Are You Ready for the Urban Future?" The Gospel Coalition, May 28, 2013, http://thegospelcoalition.org/blogs/tgc/2013/05/28/are-you-ready-for-cities/.
6. Stephen Um and Justin Buzzard, *Why Cities Matter* (Wheaton: IL, Crossway, 2013), Kindle edition, Introduction.

7. Jeff Nesbit, "Study of Census Data Finds a Segregated America, Especially for Blacks," *U.S. News Weekly*, July 24, 2012, www.usnews.com/news/blogs/at-the-edge/2012/07/24/study-of-census-data-finds-a-segregated-america-especially-for-blacks.

8. Erik Eckholm, "Southern Baptists Set for a Notable First," *New York Times*, June, 18, 2012, www.nytimes.com/2012/06/18/us/southern-baptists-set-to-elect-their-first-black-leaderhtml?pagewanted=all &_r=2&.

Chapter 9: For Our Kids

1. John A. Garraty and Eric Foner, eds., "March on Washington," in *The Reader's Companion to American History* (Boston: MA, Houghton Mifflin, 1991), www.history.com/topics/march-on-washington.

2. Martin Luther King Jr., "I Have a Dream," American Rhetoric: Top 100 Speeches, www.americanrhetoric.com/speeches/mlkihaveadream.htm.

3. Wendy Wang, "The Rise of Intermarriage," Pew Research Social and Demographic Trends, February, 16 2012, http://www.pewsocialtrends.org/2012/02/16/the-rise-of-intermarriage/.

4. Trillia Newbell, "Locals React to Ban on Interracial Couples at Kentucky Church," *Knoxville News-Sentinel*, December 2, 2011, www.knoxnews.com/news/2011/dec/02/locals-react-to-interracial-ban-at-ky-church/.

5. John Piper, "Racial Harmony and Interracial Marriage," Desiring God, January 16, 2005, www.desiringgod.org/searches/interracial%20marriage?utf8=%E2%9C%93.

6. Edward Gilbreath, *Reconciliation Blues: A Black Evangelical's Inside View of White Christianity* (Downers Grove, IL, 2006); Anthony Bradley, *Aliens in the Promised Land: Why Minority Leadership Is Overlooked in White Christian Churches and Institutions* (Phillipsburg, NJ: P&R, 2013); John Piper, *Bloodlines: Race, Cross, and the Christian* (Wheaton, IL: Crossway, 2011).

7. Charles Wesley, "O for a Thousand Tongues to Sing," 1739.

ACKNOWLEDGMENTS

THIS IS THE PAGE I HAVE BEEN most anticipating. The number of people and organizations that have expressed support and encouragement to me and for this project has been overwhelming.

Thank you to my past and present pastors for your support and encouragement throughout this process. You are a blessing to me and a constant reminder of God's goodness and faithfulness. And thank you to my church that has spurred me on and for our many years of service together.

Thank you, Jemar Tisby, Kristie Anyabwile, and Craig Cooper for your thoughtful encouragement and feedback during the beginning stages of the project. And thank you, Shannon, Bridget, and Lola for reading the very first proposal I had ever written.

I'm not sure if I would have been able to write this book without the prayers of my girlfriends. Thank you for praying for me and writing notes of encouragement Amy, Elizabeth, Allison, and Krista.

Thank you, Amy and Lillian, for contributing to *United*, for your love, and for your friendship all these years. Who would have known that a moment in a cafeteria would lead to rich friendships and now this book? You are a forever blessing to me. I love you!

Holly Kisly, thank you stopping me at the True Woman conference and being so interested in my writing and ultimately acquiring this project. I'm so blessed. Thank you, Rene Hanebutt, for your faithfulness and hard work. It has been wonderful getting to work with you and to now count you as a friend. Thank you, Lydia Brownback, for making this project the best it could be. I was overjoyed when I got word that you would be editing it. I can't thank you enough.

A special thank you to The Gospel Coalition, specifically to Collin Hansen, Kathleen Nielson, and John Starke for taking such an interest in this topic and my writing. Kathleen, thank you for your example as a woman grounded in theology and femininity. I pray I could be like you. Collin, you have been a real joy to work with. You've challenged and stretched me to think deeply. Thank you, Trevin Wax, for your interest in my perspective, for wanting others to know, and for your continued support and friendship. Thank you to the Reformed African American Network. Most grateful for the founders Phillip Holmes and Jemar Tisby. Thank you, Desiring God, specifically Tony Reinke and Jonathan Parnell, for also taking such an interest in the topic of race and racial harmony. Your love for the body of Christ is remarkable. Tony, I have learned much from our interactions. I am confident I understand the Scriptures and how to read and handle the text more skillfully as a result. I have benefited greatly from your ministry and thank God for you! Thank you, Pastor John Piper, for your continued support and kindness to me. As you know, there would not be *United* if there wasn't first *Bloodlines*. You are a blessing, and your ministry has been the tool (along with the Bible) the Lord has used to teach me more about Himself.

Erik Wolgemuth is an all-star agent. I'm not sure how he could be matched. Erik, thank you for your diligence, professionalism, wisdom, and friendship. You are a pure joy to work with. Although I will be learning how to write for the rest of my life, I am a better writer as a result of our interactions. Thank you to the entire Wolgemuth and Associates team.

Thank you, Mom, Tennion, and Barb, for your support and care. I love you. Dad and Alicia would be excited! Tennion, thank you for your many phone calls and public love. Thank you, Mum and Dad Newbell, for allowing me a space to write and edit. I love you.

Perhaps the most significant person I'd like to thank, besides the Lord, would be my husband. Thern, there aren't enough words to thank you for your support and wisdom, guidance and leadership. Thank you for allowing me time to write and, most importantly, spend time with the Lord. You are my hero. I love you and the kids so very much.

May God be glorified through this little book. Thank You, Lord. I love You!

LETTERS TO A
BIRMINGHAM JAIL

978-0-802 4-1196-9

Letters to a Birmingham Jail is a collection of essays written by men of various ethnicities and ages, yet all are committed to the centrality of the gospel, nudging us to pursue Christ exalting diversity. The gospel demands justice in all its forms - spiritual and physical. This was a truth that Dr. King fought and gave his life for, and this is a truth that these modern day "drum majors for justice" continue to beat.

Also available as an ebook

MOODY
PUBLISHERS

www.MoodyPublishers.com